Social Dance in the Mormon West

Social Dance in the Mormon West

by Craig R. Miller
with an Essay by Larry V. Shumway

Published by
THE UTAH ARTS COUNCIL
2000

Copyright: 2000, Utah Arts Council, Salt Lake City, Utah
All Rights Reserved

Library of Congress Catalog Card Number: 98-61252
Social Dance in the Mormon West / Craig R. Miller with an Essay by Larry V. Shumway
Edited by Carol Edison and David Stanley
Design: Kinde Nebeker Design/Robin Kroll
ISBN: 0-9623975-4-7

Cover photos: Clockwise from top left: Pattie Richards, on accordion, teaches the old-time dance repertoire to dancers Gus Horn and Jill Webster, Annie Hatch, photographer; the Wasatch Mountain Club, photo courtesy of University of Utah Marriott Library Special Collections, Wasatch Mountain Club Collection; Utah Pioneer Centennial Celebration at St. George, 1947, photo courtesy of the Utah State Historical Society; Virgin River Valley, photo by Craig R. Miller; First Family Orchestra of Gunlock, photo courtesy of the Lynne Clark Historical Collection, Rose McAllister, donor.

Title page photo: Saltair, courtesy of the Utah State Historical Society.

Back cover photos: Saltair, photo by Wilkes, courtesy of the Utah State Historical Society; Craig R. Miller, photo by Busath Photography.

Companion Pieces:
"An Old-Time Utah Dance Party: Field Recording of Social Dance from the Mormon West" on cassette and compact disc
An Old-Time Utah Dance Party: Sheet Music and Dance Steps

The Utah Arts Council, a state agency, is a division of the Department of Community and Economic Development.

Michael O. Leavitt, Governor; David A. Winder, Director of DCED; Bonnie H. Stephens, Director of UAC; Board Members: Sara Lee Gibb, Chair; Fred M. Babcock, Vice-Chair; Meg Brady, Ann Cullimore Decker, Fred Esplin, Neil Hadlock, Jerry Holyoak, John T. Nielsen, Robert Olpin, Kathy Peterson, Floyd Rigby, Neila C. Seshachari, Joanne Schiebler.

Folk Arts Program Coordinator: Carol Edison; Folk Arts Advisory Panel: Meg Brady, Chair; William Afeaki, Forrest Cuch, Stephen Epperson, Karen Krieger, Liz Montague, Jill Terry Rudy.

This is a project of the Utah Arts Council with support from the Salt Lake County Centennial Commission and the Utah State Centennial Commission.

Dancing on the summit of Mt. Timpanogas! Annual hikes to the top of Mt. Timpanogas have been a tradition for the Wasatch Mountain Club and for BYU students and alumni since the turn of the 20th century. These hikers celebrate their reaching the summit by striking a dance pose for the camera. Photo reproduced with permission of Michael R. Kelsey.

TABLE OF CONTENTS

PREFACE AND ACKNOWLEDGEMENTS	1
AN OVERVIEW OF DANCE	
The Role of Dance in Society	5
Dance in the Mormon West, 1847-2000	6
FOUNDATIONS OF THE TRADITION:	
DANCING AMONG THE MORMON PIONEERS	
by Larry V. Shumway	11
Nineteenth-Century American Views on Dancing	12
Nauvoo Period:	
The Church Takes a Positions on Dancing	14
Dancing on the Plains	16
Dancing in Utah Territory	18
Dancing to the Fiddle	24

THE STORY OF OLD-TIME MORMON DANCE	
Settling Deseret	27
Building Community through Dance	28
The Round Dance Revolution	31
The Golden Years of Mormon Dance	35
Origins of Old-Time Tunes and Dances	36
The Old-Time Dance Repertoire in Contemporary Times	42
Orderville: The Evolution of Dance in One Small Town	45
Twentieth-Century Technologies	49
Utah's Dance Halls	51
The Future of Old-Time Dance	54
SOURCES CITED	56
INDEX	57

Preface and Acknowledgements

In 1985 I began conducting research to learn about the culture of the Mormon West through a study of the region's dance traditions. For members of The Church of Jesus Christ of Latter-day Saints (the Mormons), social dance has always played an important role in building community. During pioneer times, dance was used to build social cohesion, and Mormon leaders made sure that each new settlement, from Mexico to Canada, had its own supply of dance musicians. A century and a half later, this heritage of community-based music and dance still survived in many Mormon communities throughout the Intermountain West. It is this heritage that I sought to understand.

While several master's theses and articles had been written on the history of dance in Utah, my project was designed to salvage what was left of the old-time dance and music repertoire while people still remembered how important dance and music had been in their lives and in the growth of their communities. As a folklorist for the Utah Arts Council, I traveled around the state recording dance music, collecting oral histories and absorbing impressions from the many people who had dedicated their lives to fulfilling their communities' needs for music and dance. Most of the musicians that I recorded ranged in age from sixty-five to ninety. None of their performances were recorded in a sound studio, but instead in the familiar setting of home or at actual community dances.

In 1996, the Utah Arts Council produced a compilation of these recordings entitled *An Old-Time Utah Dance Party: Field Recordings of Social Dance Music from the Mormon West*. Guided by the stories told by musicians and dancers, I organized the selections to re-create a community dance party like those typically held throughout the region before the advent of the radio, phonograph, or other modern forms of mass communication.

Researching and trying to understand the significance of social dance in the Mormon West has involved a great deal of detective work. It required searching for clues in far-flung places and in unexpected forms that often appear unrelated. An old song that seemed out of place among a band's repertoire of popular country-and-western tunes, crumbling arches spotted in a long-abandoned field that on closer inspection surrounded a cracked concrete dance floor, a few old photographs in a family album, the name of a dance written in the faded ink of a pioneer journal—these provided the keys that helped me begin to understand this heritage.

Sam Chidester, the fiddling bishop of Wayne County, poses outside his home. Photo courtesy of Lell Heaps.

Catherine Garner, accordion, and Genevieve Johnston, bass ukulele, play old-time dance music with the Hooper Hometown Players. They grew up on a farm in Hooper, Weber County. Together with their five sisters, the Parker Sisters sing for various church and community functions. Photo by Carol Edison, 1991.

One pitfall I tried to avoid was clouding history with modern interpretations, biases and misunderstandings. I have tried to remember that the role of dance in community settings and society's attitudes toward social dance have changed dramatically over the last 150 years. Since dance is under-appreciated today, it would be easy to project our modern values onto previous times. Stoically posed photographs from the nineteenth century give the misimpression that life in those days was stern and rigid, more "black and white" than the present. Studying these photographs, it would be easy to assume that dance was insignificant in the "survive or die" mentality of the frontier West and that early settlers must have been too sensible to waste time in such frivolity.

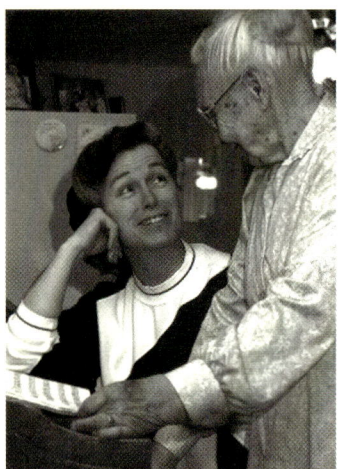

Carole Barlow (seated) learns the heritage of old-time piano music which Verna Black has kept alive at community dances in Arizona's Colorado City. Photo by Keith Jones, 1994.

Another pitfall lies in the tendency to let the distance of time lead to a romantic and somewhat unrealistic re-invention of our ancestors and how they faced life. Dissatisfaction with the complexities of modern life can lure us to simplify history and view the past as an idyllic time when social dances were conducted in mythological proportions of grace, reserve and community unity.

The truth can be found in the vibrant memories of the people who lived during these earlier times. Memories that were recorded in journals or passed on in oral forms from generation to generation reveal our ancestors as real human beings consumed in the experience of creating a new society in the American West. Firsthand stories full of reverence, idealism, and authority are balanced with levity, disillusionment and debate. The stories bridge the gap of time, help us understand the role of social dance for Utahns and make our ancestors human, not so dissimilar from us today.

But if the values of our pioneer ancestors are to be perpetuated, let us pay tribute to Kenner C. Kartchner, the Forest Service fiddler who evoked the muse of music to calm range wars on the Arizona frontier, and Sam Chidester, the fiddling bishop of Wayne County, who traveled far and wide to provide music for the farthest-flung settlements. Let us remember LeRoy and Weltha Thacker who, with a baby in a shoebox and a violin between them, crossed the Uintah Mountains by buggy to homestead the Uintah Basin and then played for community dances for the next 50 years. And let us also remember Iva Williams Wood, a woman who built the Cobblecrest dance hall in Kanarraville in the 1930s, a place that 60 years later is still packed with dancers and brimming with music on summer Saturday evenings.

Our ancestors had a thirst, a love for music and dance

The Cobblecrest outdoor dance hall in Kanarraville is often packed with dancers on a summer Saturday evening. Photo by Craig R. Miller, 1995.

that few people appreciate or even understand today. So let us also thank the living practitioners of this dance and music tradition who love their heritage and unselfishly carry it on for the benefit of the next generation. The seven Parker sisters of Hooper still bless their community with music. For fifty years Rosy Jessop of Bluffdale called the dances his father called before him, and Carole Barlow follows in the footsteps of Verna Black and Maryette Carling, who throughout their long lives played for Colorado City dances that have changed very little over the course of the twentieth century.

Dance historian Laraine Miner revives the old-time dance repertoire for monthly community dances in Salt Lake County. Photo by Craig R. Miller, 1999.

I entered this project as an outsider who was drawn to the subject by a love for the music, the dances and the people who created and perpetuated them. So to fully understand these traditions, I turned to Larry Shumway, Associate Professor of Ethnomusicology at Brigham Young University. In addition to his academic training, Larry had the great fortune to grow up immersed in the religion, the culture and the traditions of Utah's old-time dance musicians. A descendant of pioneers and the grandson of legendary fiddler Kenner C. Kartchner, Larry is also a fiddler and as such has a unique vantage point in commenting on this history and heritage.

As I look back on this project, I realize it is an uncommon blessing to have the opportunity to work with people of advanced age who are still keen in their knowledge and enthusiasm for life. So much can be learned by just listening to them. This project has depended upon the knowledge and kindness of many people who were generous in sharing their experiences, memories and talents. Some have already passed on to another life, but I extend thanks to all who offered help and encouragement.

I especially wish to thank Laraine Miner for introducing me to Utah dance in 1983, and for sharing with me her master's thesis, "Early Utah Dances." Laraine has taken this project to its next logical step by organizing community dances with live musicians and teaching dance workshops to Utah schoolchildren.

I also thank the Utah Humanities Council for sponsoring over fifty lectures on this topic that I gave through their Speakers Bureau. These programs took me to communities across the state where I met people like Robert and Lyndia Carter, who shared with me their own historical research. I also met Sagebrush Flanigan after a lecture in Cedar City when he gave me copies of the John Perry Orchestra, originally recorded in 1944. Thanks also to Lell Heaps, who gave me photographs and tape recordings of his grandfather, Sam Chidester; to the Lynne Clark Photographic Studios of St.

Forgotten remnants of the Shady Dell outdoor dance hall lie in a secluded grove by the Sevier River, six miles north of Big Rock, Candy Mountain. Photo by Craig R. Miller, 1989.

Larry Shumway with mother Merle, holds the violin his grandfather Kenner C. Kartchner played. Photo by Craig R. Miller, 1987.

George for collecting historical photographs from Utah's Dixie and for giving me permission to use them in this publication; and to Keith Jones, who accompanied me on field trips and lectures. His legacy lives in the photographs he contributed to this publication and in his unfettered wit and love for dance which is still an inspiration to many, especially me. And truthfully, this project never would have reached completion without the patient encouragement of Carol Edison, my friend and colleague who coordinates the Utah Arts Council Folk Arts Program.

I am indebted to all the generous people whom I met while conducting this research around the state. They shared with me their time and knowledge, historical recordings and photographs. There are too many to thank individually here, but their stories are told in the pages that follow. I consider them all to be my friends.

— *Craig R. Miller*

Clockwise from top:
Hooper musicians play for an old-time dance at Antelope Island State Park. Pictured are Genevieve Johnston, ukulele, Bonnie Call, violin, Catherine Garner, accordion, and Margie Kite, guitar. Photo by Craig R. Miller, 1995.

The Fielding Garr Ranch in Antelope Island State Park sponsors a summer program of old-time music and dance featuring musicians from the community of Hooper, situated in Weber County on the shore of the Great Salt Lake. Photo by Keith Jones, 1995.

Utah Pioneer Centennial Celebration at St. George. A 1947 revival of the early Mormon pioneer dances. Photo courtesy of the Utah State Historical Society.

An Overview of Dance

The Role of Dance in Society

Why is it that in any city on a given night there may be classical ballet on stage, a folk-dance performance in an ethnic church, a political fund-raising dance at the university, a pow-wow at the convention center, a social dance in a barrio cantina, a children's rehearsal for a founder's day pageant performance, and a teenage couple dancing under the stars in a dark parking lot to tunes played over their car radio? In each of those varied scenes dance is fulfilling a basic human need. Dance can reinforce a community's aesthetic ideals, build cultural identity, communicate political and social relationships, provide recreation, educate our young to a system of values, and provide the context for the courtship rituals that keep society renewed. Such are the powerfully human expressions of dance.

Dance seems a common, straightforward component of modern life, yet its functions remain elusive. Over the ages, dance has served different purposes for different cultures, and it can address a variety of different needs even within one society. As a result, an understanding of the form, context and function of dance expression provides great insight into the culture and the people themselves.

History demonstrates that dance is one of the most powerful means of expressing cultural identity. Consequently conquering nations have repeatedly turned to prohibitions of dance and other forms of cultural expression in attempts to intimidate, subjugate or assimilate those conquered. In our own region of the American West and as late as the early twentieth century, laws were passed banning certain forms of American Indian dance for fear that dance could fan the flames of cultural discontent and foment popular uprisings. One nearby example is the United States government's outlawing of the sacred Ute Sun Dance from 1904 until 1934.

But because music and dance can also be powerful expressions of community and individualism, they are, of all forms of cultural expression, the hardest to legislate or control. Despite a history of suppressive efforts by governments and people in authority, dance and other forms of artistic expression continue to be among the most democratic expressions of people everywhere. When people face cultural pressures, they often turn to dance to express frustration and build community support and unity of direction. When people face injustice, they dance in defiance. When a society experiences losses and sadness, dance becomes therapy. And when a society experiences prosperity and peace, dance becomes a celebration of stability and bounty. Neither one dance nor a whole repertoire of dances can express all of these situations adequately, so as society changes from one era to another, so change the context, the form, and the cultural significance of specific dances and of dance in general.

The nineteenth-century Mormon pioneers (members of The Church of Jesus Christ of Latter-day Saints) who settled the Intermountain West experienced periods of great change as they established new communities on the western frontier. The story of the culture they built, understood through one of their strongest cultural expressions, social dance, is the story we tell here.

Dance in the Mormon West, 1847-2000

DURING THE LATE NINETEENTH and early twentieth centuries, social dancing flourished in communities originally settled by Mormon pioneers in the Intermountain West. According to old journal and newspaper accounts, community dances were the most popular form of recreation throughout the region. In Utah, the heart of Mormon settlement, a style of old-time music and dance developed which reflected the character and values of its settlers.

At the core of this style is a body of music and dance that was established before radio and phonograph introduced popular fox-trot and swing tunes, before physical education instructors taught classroom folk dance, before professional callers interpreted modern square dance, and before social and folk dance forms were adapted to stage performance. These old-time dances include quadrilles, Virginia reels, and those known regionally as round dances.

Senior citizens dance once a week in St. George. Here they perform the old-time schottische. Photo by Craig R. Miller, 1989.

Some, like the Virginia reel and quadrilles, were brought to the area by pioneers who danced between covered wagons during evenings on the trail. Some, like the schottische and the waltz, were brought by immigrants directly from Scandinavia and western Europe. Others, like the waltz quadrille and the Baltimore glide, were nationally popular ballroom dances of the nineteenth century, and still others, like the varsouvienne, entered the repertoire from Spanish-speaking communities of the American Southwest.

In cities, in rural communities and on frontier ranches throughout the region, social dances were an ever-present weave in the social fabric from the pioneer times of the 1840s and '50s until the end of World War II. Although twentieth-century technology ushered in changes in repertoire and setting, the function of community dances remained pretty much the same throughout the Big Band Era of the 1930s and '40s—a time when social dancing reached its peak in popularity. In response to this mania for dance, indoor and outdoor private dance halls sprang up across the region, establishing a presence on the landscape that has persisted to the twenty-first century.

After World War II, the West followed national social, economic and technological trends that gradually changed the form, function and context of recreation in America. Entertainment became more accessible on an individual rather than a community basis and more accessible for spectators than for participants. Passive forms of recreation like cinema, television and, later, home videos surpassed social activities like dance as the main sources of entertainment. Watching team sports filled the need for community-based social activities. But team competition encourages segregation of the sexes, age groups, and whole generations, and therefore contributes to the loss of community cohesion. As community values and entertainment opportunities changed, the popularity of social dance faded in America and in the Intermountain West.

Throughout the 1960s, Gold and Green Balls kept LDS church dances alive, and in the '70s and '80s, high-school proms provided opportunities for teenagers to dance at least once a year. But the increased generational segregation of American society became visible on the dance floor as well. The older generation was totally alienated by the new aesthetics of popular music and dance, which reflected in turn the social and political upheavals of the late twentieth century and brought popular culture into direct collision with hometown values. In the late 1960s, dancing to rock and roll was banned from the Brigham Young University campus and subsequently from LDS church dances all around the region. Eventually social dancing disappeared almost entirely from church-sponsored activities and the controversy over "rock dancing" was avoided completely.

On the main street in Torrey, Wayne County, across an irrigation ditch lined with tall cottonwood trees, stands the Big Apple outdoor dance hall. Photo by Craig R. Miller, 1987.

Pattie Richards and Cory Webster play for an old-time dance at the Utah State Fair. Photo by Craig R. Miller, 1994.

Dance historian Laraine Miner personally experienced the rock-and-roll dance ban at BYU: "When I told my paternal grandfather my dismay at not being able to do these dances on the BYU campus, he said 'Oh, that's not so bad. I can remember when they wouldn't even let us do the Waltz. We could only Square Dance. Then when they finally let us do the Waltz, they would come around with a ruler to make sure there was the proper distance between partners.'"[1]

Thirty years after the arrival of rock and roll, at the end of the twentieth century, an increased interest in alternative styles of popular dance entered the region. Contemporary Nashville-style country-and-western music gained popularity in both urban and rural areas of Utah, although purists and old-timers claimed it was neither "country" nor "western." It inspired a renewed interest in social dancing and introduced several dance forms which were new to the region. One was the Texas two-step, an old-style couple dance which originated in Texas but gained national popularity in the 1980s through Hollywood movies like *Urban Cowboy*, and in addition to the standard regional variation of western swing, popular in the Intermountain West since mid-century, new swing variants such as East Coast and West Coast swing were taught in local dance clubs.

Western line dance also gained popularity. A dance form that grew out of rock and roll and the choreography of Broadway musicals and hit Hollywood films, it was popular in singles bars, senior centers or just about any place where people could enjoy dancing without the need to find a partner. In fact, with the help of technology, local dance instructors could scan the internet from their home computers, download the newest western line-dance choreography, and teach the dance— all on the same day that a star vocalist released a new hit song! By the end of the 1990s, there already existed hundreds of western line-dance internet sites around the world containing information on everything from etiquette on the dance floor to choreographies that generally began with a description like "4-wall, 40-count dance."

By the end of the twentieth century in Utah, music and dance were even beginning to cross ethnic and cultural boundaries. Salsa revived the faded popularity of Latin dance, and classic rock and roll is now accepted, whether performed at an upscale Utah Symphony gala or in a foreign language at an ethnic festival. Fads like ska and slam dancing also had a passing impact on some dance floors, providing further evidence that social dance in the region has expanded to reflect a greater diversity of lifestyles and allegiances to different facets of popular culture.

Despite these changes, the old-time dance repertoire still exists as orchestras and dance bands across Utah cling to the traditions and values of their heritage. In a few rare instances, community dance still functions pretty much unchanged, providing intergenerational interaction and the opportunity to learn and practice social graces. More commonly, these community-based traditions are carried on within the family or exist as treasured relics of heritage incorporated into some other context— an Old Folks' Day celebration, a pioneer reenactment or a senior-citizen party. In a variety of forms, this product of generations of devoted dancers is still alive, still remembered and still guarded by the dancers and musicians who loved it best. Perhaps old-time social dance will still be here when society has tired of popular fads and passing technologies. Perhaps it will again be fashionable for communities to support local musicians who create their own music and to participate once again in social activities rather than simply observe as spectators.

When society is ready to look to its heritage for inspiration and guidance, these dances will be ready. In preparation for that time, we offer this history of the tradition and a summary of its form and function within Utah culture. Perhaps a future generation, maybe even ours, will find strength and continuity by turning to the same old-time community social dance that helped to shape the culture of the Mormon West.

The outdoor dance hall in Kanosh exhibits classic architectural features including an arched entryway, perimeter walls, a social area, complete with fire pit, and, of course, a large concrete floor for social dancing. Photo by Carol Edison, 1983.

Clockwise from top left:

Merle K. Shumway, member of the St. Johns Guitar and Mandolin Club, 1962. Photo courtesy of the Merle Shumway family collection.

Arizona fiddlers Kenner C. Kartchner and Claude Youngblood played for ranch and community dances on the Arizona frontier. Photo courtesy of the Merle Shumway family collection.

A group of Orderville pioneers gathers to be honored in the old Orderville Ward House. In addition to religious services, the ward house was the site of many community gatherings including fine dramatic productions. Notice the hand-painted curtain on the stage. The ward house was also the site for social dances and all the pews or chairs would be pushed against the walls to make room for dancing on the fine wooden floor. Photo courtesy of Rena Tait.

Foundations of the Tradition: Dancing Among the Mormon Pioneers

By Larry V. Shumway

The organized movement of thousands of Mormon pioneers across the plains to Utah, beginning in 1846, must surely qualify as one of the great migrations in human history. That so many were willing to make the journey in the face of hardship, deprivation and uncertainty of their destination and fate calls forth deep admiration for their determination and gumption. Yet stories of hardship often overshadow description of the pioneers' recreational activities, which lifted their spirits and rejuvenated them physically—activities that centered around singing and dancing. Brigham Young, who organized this vast operation, is reported to have told the people at Winter Quarters, early in the trek, "I want you to sing and dance and forget your troubles. We must think of the future that lies ahead and the work which is ours."[1] The pioneers did just that and they "had many a dance while on the plains."

In her autobiography, Jesse Belle Stirling Pack describes the nightly entertainment:

> We traveled all day on the plains and if we could not get to water, we traveled all night. When we would camp we gathered buffalo chips and wood where we could and built our fire and cooked a little bacon. Then the boys would get their fiddles and we would clear off the brush and dance and sing Scotch songs. Then we would sing hymns and have prayers and go to bed.[3]

Fiddle music for dancing, perhaps fiddle-accompanied singing (hence the reference to "Scotch" songs since Ms. Pack was from Dundee, Scotland), and hymn singing all preceded evening prayers. Joined by their leaders, the group's participation in music and dance undoubtedly took their minds off the cares and worries of the day and provided relief from the tedium and fatigue of their journey.

Nineteenth-Century American Views on Dancing

GIVEN THE PROMINENCE OF DANCING among the Mormon pioneers, it is interesting that in the history of American recreation, perhaps no activity has come in for more condemnation and censure than dancing and its accompanying music. Moralists, Christian clerics and other social arbiters have ever been in the forefront of this criticism because they have perceived dancing to be not only frivolous and worldly but, more dangerously, a quick step toward degradation and sin. At best dancing was seen as a distraction from more serious things; at worst it led to sure damnation. Given the strict Christian underpinnings of Mormon pioneer society, it may seem remarkable that from the outset dancing was such a widespread, church-sanctioned activity. This is even more surprising since a very large number of the early Mormons came from strict New England religious traditions in which dancing was forbidden.

But there were competing points of view at the time, for dancing was a widespread, popular activity in mid-nineteenth-century America. One view was that dancing was good physical exercise which would develop both muscles and stamina. Another was that dancing developed grace in one's carriage and movement which in turn led to polished social manners. Yet another held that dancing eased the way for social interaction in an atmosphere of conviviality and community solidarity. It is clear that before they began their westward trek in 1846, all of these competing views were present among the Mormons. Elizabeth Whitney, wife of a prominent early church leader, described her childhood:

> I was the eldest child, and grew up in an atmosphere of love and tenderness. I received all the advantages of education, such as young ladies usually enjoyed at that time, and was taught dancing among other things, which, in the religious world in that day, was not considered orthodox. My parents were not members of any church, and they wished me to enjoy life, and thought dancing added grace and easiness to one's manner.[4]

The opposite attitude toward dance within early Mormon society was reported by Benjamin F. Johnson, who was threatened for supposedly participating in dancing in Kirtland, Ohio:

> In the early spring of 1838 an effort was made by the local authorities to draw the line of fellowship on practices which then seemed tending to demoralize, among which was dancing and late night associations. . . . I had never danced, and rarely attended a party, but from some cause my name was in the list, and I received notice to appear and answer.[5]

Aaron Nelson's String Group, St. George, Washington County, circa late 1860s. Aaron Nelson's String Group furnished music for many different occasions dating from the late 1860s. They played for dances in St. George, Washington and Santa Clara. Early personnel consisted of three "Joes"—Joseph Fordham, Joseph Worthen and Joseph Kirkham, violinists—William Nelson, flutist, and the director, Aaron Nelson, cellist. Others who played in the Nelson orchestra later were William Nelson (son of William and grandson of Aaron Nelson) and Joseph Cooper. Photo courtesy of the Lynne Clark Historical Collection, St. George, Nellie Gubler, donor.

A depiction of the weekly cotillion parties in Salt Lake City typically held during the 1860s and '70s. Photo courtesy of the Utah State Historical Society.

The Pine Valley Chapel is the classic example of the all-purpose Mormon ward house which held community dances in addition to religious services. Photo by Tom Carter, 1981.

Nauvoo Period: The Church Takes a Position on Dancing

SINCE DANCING PARTIES WERE COMMON during the Nauvoo period (1839-46), the controversy continued. Things were brought to a head in 1844 by an eloquent letter to the editor sent to the church publication *Times and Seasons* requesting a clarification of the church's stand on dancing; it was signed simply "a father and elder in Israel."

> DEAR SIR: As you are placed as a watchman in Zion, and your opinion is respected by the members of the church, I should be very much gratified by your informing me, and not only me, but the public, through the medium of your valuable paper, the Times and Seasons, what your views are in regard to balls and dancing, as it has lately existed in our city.... I feel desirous to know what to teach my children.... There are many others who possess the same feelings as myself, and who would feel highly gratified by an expression from you relative to this subject.[6]

The reply, written probably by the editor, John Taylor, was included in the same issue. It began with the observation "that there existed on the minds of the religious community, a great deal of unnecessary superstition in relation to dancing" and then outlined more or less the views noted above: "... but like all other athletic exercises, it has a tendency to invigorate the system and to promote health ... having a tendency to add to the grace and dignity of man, by enabling him to have a more easy and graceful attitude." He concludes by reiterating the church's neutrality toward dancing as an activity, focusing instead on the contexts of time and place:

> As an abstract principle ... we have no objections to [dancing]; but when it leads people into bad company and causes them to keep untimely hours, it has a tendency to enervate and weaken the sys-

tem, and lead to profligate and intemperate habits. And so far as it does this, so far it is injurious to society, and corrupting to the morals of youth. Solomon says that "there is a time to dance": but that time is not at eleven or twelve o'clock at night, nor at one, two, three or four o'clock in the morning.[7]

It seems, then, that popular opinion acknowledged that dancing had positive physical and social effects if carefully monitored and controlled by church authorities. Furthermore, as illustrated in the scriptures, dancing could be a "part of the service to God." These were all persuasive arguments in favor of the practice of dancing. Yet these benefits could only be enjoyed in the proper atmosphere and, evidently, that atmosphere was lacking in some of the dances around Nauvoo. This is illustrated by the reminiscence of a young girl denied the opportunity of attending a dancing party because of a warning to her father from Joseph Smith about the dubious company in attendance:

> During the winter of 1843 . . . some of the young gentlemen got up a series of dancing parties to be held at the [Nauvoo] mansion once a week. . . . I had to stay at home, as my father had been warned by the Prophet to keep his daughter away from there, because of the blacklegs and certain ones of questionable character who attended there. . . .[8]

After the assassination of Joseph Smith in 1844, Brigham Young became the leader of the church. In these sad and grim times, dancing was almost forgotten as the people's attention was called to other, more pressing things. But the love of dance never died, nor did the controversy surrounding it. Dancing did have the potential for worldliness and excessive frivolity and tended to distract people from the real and demanding needs of the hour. On the other hand, within certain bounds and constraints, dancing was a commendable practice that offered exercise and sociability, and engendered social graces. After much deliberation, Brigham Young concluded that dancing had the capability to build a sense of community and social cohesion and to buoy up people's spirits. He realized that under appropriate circumstances and in the right atmosphere, dancing could be extremely beneficial because of its strong potential to uplift the people's spirits. This rationale gave dancing a spiritual and intellectual affirmation which enabled the pioneers to continue its practice and to enjoy all of its benefits, while at the same time severely limiting any ill effects it might have on an appropriate piety. Thus, the person who shaped the post-Nauvoo Mormon view of dancing was none other than Brigham Young himself— a man who had been heard to say earlier "that to listen to the sound of a violin was an unforgivable sin in his father's household" but who later "became a wonderful dancer [who] loved all sorts of art and music."[9]

Dan and Louis Crawford played for dances in the communities in Zion Canyon, circa 1890. Photo by Crawford of Springdale, Washington County. Photo courtesy of the Lynne Clark Historical Collection, St. George, Cy Gifford, donor.

Dancing on the Plains

WITH BRIGHAM YOUNG'S APPROVAL, dancing became a favorite activity in Nauvoo and later around the campfires of the migration as the Mormons fled westward from their persecutors. Thus, from the beginning of the trek in 1846, the Mormon pioneers danced to lift their spirits, often in the outdoors and even during inclement weather:

> While in Nauvoo, [William] Pitt had organized a splendid band and was with the Mormon pioneers when they crossed the ice of the Mississippi in the cold days of February 1846. During the march of the pioneers his band cheered the pilgrims, and while in Winter Quarters, Pitt's band gladdened the people's hearts through the long and dreary winter. After encampment was made and the toils of the day were over, the snow would be scraped away, a huge fire (or several of them) kindled within the wagoned enclosure, and there, to the inspiring music of Pitt's band, song and dance often beguiled the exiles into forgetfulness of their trials and discomforts.[10]

Enterprise Orchestra in front of John Day's store, Enterprise, Washington County, 1910. L to R: John Day, Rhoda Crawford, Jim Huitt, Edwin Hall, Pearl Eliker, Emily Hall, Estella Hall, James Hall. Photo courtesy of the Lynne Clark Historical Collection, St. George, Olive Truman, donor.

Realizing they could not get prepared soon enough to complete the trek to the West, the pioneers set up several temporary settlements across Iowa. The main one was Winter Quarters, on the bank of the Missouri River near what is now Omaha. They remained there until the spring of 1847. During this time, Pitt's band provided much music for general entertainment as well as dancing, even earning some money playing several concerts in nearby towns.[11]

In June, 1846, the United States government recruited some five hundred Mormon men to aid in the war with Mexico. The day before the Mormon Battalion was to leave, they were given a rousing send-off dance that was described by Col. Thomas Kane:

> There was no sentimental affectation at their leave-taking. The afternoon before was appropriated to a farewell ball; and a more merry dancing rout I have never seen, though the company went without refreshments, and their ballroom was of the most primitive [a bowery]. . . . [The church leaders], the gravest and most trouble worn, seemed the most anxious of any to be first to throw off the burden of heavy thoughts. Their leading off the dancing in a great double cotillion, was the signal bade the festivity commence. To the canto of debonair violins, the cheer of horns, the jingle of sleigh bells, and the jovial snoring of the tambourine, they did dance . . . the spirited and scientific displays of our venerated and merry grandparents, who were not above following the fiddle to the Foxchase Inn, or Gardens of Gray's Ferry. French Fours, Copenhagen Jigs, Virginia Reels, and the like forgotten figures executed with the spirit of people too happy to be slow, or bashful, or constrained. Light hearts, lithe figures, and light feet, had it their own way from an early hour till after the sun had dipped behind the sharp sky line of the Omaha hills.[12]

The dances mentioned were those typical of pioneer times, figure dances in which couples moved through various patterns, usually touching each other only with hands and arms. Chief among these were reels and quadrilles (simple forerunner of the later square dance) which mixed people together, changing partners often, and— in the

Virginia reels in particular—giving a dancer a chance to swing a variety of partners. Dancing continued at Winter Quarters, usually accompanied by the fiddle, but still Pitt's band furnished some music:

> The brethren built a council House, and they called a meeting to dedicate it, Brother Brigham there and a number of the twelve. They talked about having a dance for those who had built it or assisted. Brother Brigham said he was going to have the first dance and his brethren with him so they would set a pattern for the rest. They called for the band, and on they came forthwith. Brother Brigham organized a number of couples and set the band to playing a tune, after which they kneeled down and prayed to the God of Heaven.... Truly I was led to say his was the way the ancient fathers praised the Lord in a dance. The floor had been made of green timber.[13]

A year later, in the spring of 1847, the pioneers resumed their journey across the plains. The dust, drudgery and hardship that bedeviled their daily travel was often mitigated in the evening with song and dance around the campfire, sometimes between the wagons. Harriett Pulsipher recorded that "sometimes on week nights, they would clear away the brush and engage in dancing."[14] Later, Mary Culmer noted that "the people would gather around the campfire and after some singing and prayer, there would be dancing."[15] And as perhaps said best, "No matter how difficult had been the journey during the day, when dusk came and the camp had been pitched, the evening meal eaten, the weariness of the day was forgotten in a dance."[16] Certainly for the young folks there were some things which could not be postponed, and for many of them the journey represented adventure and romance with evening dances providing the opportunity for courting. In his autobiography, Aroet Hale recalled:

> Our travels across the plains was a long, tiresome trip over one thousand miles with ox teams. It was hard on old people and women with children. The young folks had enjoyment. Presidents Young and Kimball were very kind and indulgent to the young. They frequently stopped within a mile or so apart. The young would visit from one camp to the other and frequently would get music and have a good

Russell Brothers Band, St. George. Photo courtesy of the St. George Daughters of the Utah Pioneers.

> dance on the ground.... I formed an acquaintance with a young lady crossing the plains that I afterwards married.... So I did my sparking along the road. So I did not have so much to do after I got into the valley.[17]

The St. George-Pine Valley Orchestra poses after serenading the town from the back of a horse-drawn trailer on July 4, 1911. Photo courtesy of the Lynne Clark Historical Collection, St. George, LaPrele Carter, donor.

Dancing in Utah Territory

THE PIONEERS BEGAN ARRIVING in the Great Salt Lake Valley July 21, 1847 and immediately began planting, planning a city, building shelters, and preparing for the later immigrants to follow. Throughout all this enterprise, dancing continued as a favored recreational activity. Large boweries were built to accommodate public functions and these were used for dancing as well. Perhaps the best-known "party" in these boweries was the great harvest feast of August, 1848. People came to display and partake of the bounties of their harvest and to sing, dance and be merry. Eliza R. Snow records that "it was a great day for the people, one long to be remembered by those who had suffered and waited anxiously for the results of their first effort to redeem the vast interior deserts of the Great West." [18]

Soon pioneers were called to settle other places and gradually a network of communities sprang up reaching from Idaho to Nevada and Arizona. As before, dancing was very much a part of life in these communities. For lack of better places, dancing was done mainly in private homes at first, then at schoolhouses, churches, and courthouses as they were built, and finally in halls which were built primarily for dancing and other entertainments.

Though now abandoned, Kimberly was a thriving mining town in Piute County when this photograph of the Kimberly Dance Hall was taken in June, 1917. Photo courtesy of Utah State Historical Society.

In Beaver, for example, John Mathews "built his home knowing that he would be called upon to offer it for such purposes. He built partitions between certain rooms that could easily be moved, making a larger space for dancing and other functions. Needless to say, many parties were held here."[19] Although furniture and rugs had to be moved out to make room for the musicians and the dancers, that seemed a small price to pay for the great fun of a dance enjoyed by the whole community. In late 1851 the town of Fillmore built a school and held its first public dance there:

> It had one big room and was made of cottonwood logs with a large fireplace in one end, rude benches made of split logs and a dirt floor that was sprinkled and swept before each social event. On the evening of the first dance, the whole town turned out to enjoy the event. The light from the fireplace and candles revealed the happiness these early pioneers felt in thus being able to enjoy a sociable time together. Their hardships were forgotten for the time as the musicians tuned up their fiddles and banjos. The evening began with prayer, then Brother Hiram Mace, the dance master, taught some step-dancing to the younger people, after which everybody, old and young, joined in the square dancing.[20]

Of particular interest in Fillmore is the Territorial State House, built with federal money in 1855 to house the Utah Territorial Legislature. After one session, however, the legislature voted to move the territorial capital back to Salt Lake City and the building reverted to the city and Millard County. Though subsequently used for office space for the city and county and as a mission school by the Presbyterians, its top floor was particularly fine for theatricals and dancing. The top floor was a large single room with a fine pinewood floor just right for dancing. When theatricals were performed, a removable stage was set up at one end over the stairs, allowing for dramatic entrances and exits. Today this building is part of the state parks system and is still used for dances, particularly those planned by the curator, Carl Camp, in an effort to preserve pioneer dances in an ambience close to the times.

Salt Lake City, the capital as well as the center of pioneer Utah, had a rather large population and as a result structures were built specifically for entertainments like

Warm Springs Bath House, 1868. Photo courtesy of Utah State Historical Society.

WARM SPRINGS

Several miles north of the temple lot the pioneers discovered some hot-water springs. They were quick to see possibilities for a recreation area and a couple of years later the city began developing them into a park area, building bathhouses, planting grass and a number of trees. Later a dance hall was built:

> In the summer of 1850 a commodious bathhouse was built over the springs, boarding in one inner pool for women, an outer one for men and boys, with several private rooms fitted with wooden bathtubs. . . . In front of this bathhouse was an adobe cottage for the caretaker, and soon an immense dancing hall . . . built of substantial adobe, was added, with a roomy dining room equipped with kitchens, all fitted with benches and tables. Public parties and theatrical entertainments were given here, even after the completion of the Social Hall.[21]

Many socials and balls were held there, including a state ball and supper given the next summer in honor of the Chief Justice of the United States. Wedding parties used the hall as well, as Rachel Simmons recalled:

> We were married on the 18th of December, 1851, in what was called the Warm Springs Bath House. It was at that time the largest and best place for large parties. It was a fashionable place. I had as nice a wedding as could be had in those days. After the ceremony, we had [a splendid] supper then danced until next morning.[22]

Larry Shumway

Social Hall before front stairs were erected. Photo courtesy of Utah State Historical Society.

SOCIAL HALL

Perhaps the most famous dedicated recreational facility of the early pioneers was the Social Hall, built in 1852 in the center of town between South Temple and First South on State Street. It was a substantial building measuring 40 x 60 feet and made of adobe with a shingle roof. The ground floor was designed for theatricals and had a slanted floor leading down to the stage. The basement floor, on the other hand, was for dancing, parties and banquets. It was formally opened and dedicated on New Year's Day, 1853, with Heber C. Kimball calling the meeting to order and Apostle Amasa Lyman offering the dedicatory prayer. There were congratulatory speeches, musical numbers and recitations, but the "main feature of the evening" was a ball.[23] The Social Hall is perhaps better remembered for its dramatic presentations, but it was the site of many dances as well. This is illustrated by a special dance of some note, held November 29, 1855, to welcome back missionaries returning from foreign countries. Jedediah M. Grant of the First Presidency managed the proceedings: "He then led off in the dance, which he executed in right good earnest. The whole company caught the electric spark, and 'good earnest' characterized the exercises of the evening. . . . When the evening was well advanced, and the party had exercised themselves much in the dance, President Grant addressed the returned missionaries."[24]

Larry Shumway

dancing. Warm Springs Resort, built in 1850, was one of the earliest, but it was soon followed by the Social Hall, built in 1852, right in the middle of town. Dances here were the highpoint of social activity and were especially enjoyed by out-of-town visitors who were delighted to experience dancing under such favorable circumstances. Other early buildings such as the Seventies Hall and the Salt Lake Theater also housed an occasional dance, but these were typically private affairs.

The outlying pioneer settlements lagged behind Salt Lake City for some years in building halls specifically for dancing—but they were built eventually. Typical is one in Sanpete County between Moroni and Mt. Pleasant built by Niels Peter Nielsen which he appropriately called "Fiddlers Green Dance Hall":

> He then built a dance hall on his property across the road north in a thick grove of trees near the Sanpitch River. . . . It was a very large rambling structure built of lumber and so constructed that shutters enclosing the upper part of the walls could be opened. Orchestras from Mt. Pleasant, Moroni, Spring City and Fairview took turns playing for dances there, and large happy crowds attended.[25]

The son of Mormon pioneers called to settle in central Arizona, fiddler Kenner C. Kartchner poses with his frontier family. His eldest daughter Merle (top center), accompanied her father on piano and passed the family's musical heritage to her own grandchildren in Utah. Photo courtesy of Merle Shumway.

In 1876, pioneers were sent to colonize the Little Colorado River area in northern Arizona. As in other Mormon outposts, dancing was a favored community activity. Some ten years after establishing a community named

Victorian parlor entertainment included making music at home on violin, guitar and pump organ as well as viewing Stereoscopic images (woman seated at right). Pictured here is the Heber and Ellen Harrison Family of Pinto, Utah. Photo courtesy of the Lynne Clark Historical Collection, Nellie Gubler, donor.

Snowflake on Silver Creek, a tributary of the Little Colorado River, two enterprising brothers, Charlie and James Flake, built a general store. Its second story had a large open floor which came to be known as Flake Brothers' Hall. The hall was used for a variety of community activities and served, for a number of years, as one of the main places for dancing.[26]

As the pioneer period drew to a close, many more of what might be called "dedicated" dance halls were built throughout areas colonized by the Mormons. In an effort to capitalize on particularly beautiful scenery, the halls were often built next to bodies of water and were landscaped with trees, flowers and lawns in something of a pleasure-garden setting where people could come to enjoy the atmosphere, good food and entertainment. At Utah Lake, for example, dancing pavilions were built at American Fork, Pleasant Grove, Geneva, and Lincoln Beach. The largest and most beautiful of these dedicated dance halls was Saltair, the resort built on the southern shore of the Great Salt Lake in 1893. It featured a huge dancing pavilion and spectacular artificial lighting.

This depiction of social dance held in the Old Salt Lake Bowery graces the rotunda of the Utah State Capitol in Salt Lake City. Photo courtesy of Utah Arts Council.

Life on the Arizona frontier was rugged and isolated. Fiddler Kenner C. Kartchner, pictured here, supplied music for ranch dances across the Southwest as far east as Texas, and for church and community dances in Arizona and Utah. Photo courtesy of the Merle Shumway family collection.

Dancing was at the center of community social activity and whole families attended the dances. The feelings of joy and satisfaction experienced by the pioneers at such occasions were recorded in many diaries. The 1876 Fourth of July celebration in Cedar City prompted one observer to write, "Dancing by the children in the afternoon and by the adults in the evening. Peace and good order did everywhere abound throughout the whole day."[27] Of the same day in Paragonah an observer wrote, "We had a very pleasant celebration of the fourth. . . . Dancing commenced at one o'clock for the children, and in the evening adults indulged in the same way, which was kept up until a late hour. The whole affair went off very pleasantly."[28] Another diarist in Mt. Carmel in Kane County wrote, "At two p.m. the little folks assembled and occupied a few hours in dancing. Then they gave way for the more elderly ones, who occupied the time to good advantage until midnight when the dance was dismissed and all went home in peace, feeling well satisfied."[29] Dances were for the whole family, even babes in arms who were put to sleep in bedrooms, on church benches, or on beds made on the floorboards of a carriage or wagon. As another writer explained, "Often a lady was compelled to leave the floor—her baby was crying. No mother remained at home on account of children, except in cases of sickness. Babies were brought along and beds were arranged on seats with coats and shawls for coverings."[30] In this setting there was no generation gap. Children learned about being part of the community and the adult world and its expectations for them in the future.

After their arrival in the West, Mormon pioneers continued dancing with their leaders' blessing, but always with admonishment to preserve a proper atmosphere and attitude. Many journal entries record the spiritual atmosphere in which the dancing was done. Every occasion opened and closed with prayer and an unrelenting effort was made to keep out worldly influences, particularly liquor, rowdy behavior, and suspicious strangers who might bring harm to the community. This was the setting envisioned by Brigham Young: dance fulfilling its raison d'etre of providing the wholesome recreation necessary for physical, mental and social growth. The fruits of his policies regarding dancing are summarized nicely in the following remembrance by his daughter, Susa Young Gates:

> People would have had in those grinding years of toil, too few holidays and far too little of the spirit of holiday-making which is the spirit of fellowship and socialized spiritual communion, but for Brigham Young's wise policy. He manifested even more godly inspiration in his carefully regulated social activities and associated pleasure than in his pulpit exercises. He kept the people busy, gave legitimate amusements full sway and encouraged the cultivation of every power, every gift and emotion of the human soul.[31]

Around the turn of the 20th century, many dance pavilions were built on the shores of Utah and Great Salt lakes. Garfield Beach was a popular resort west of Black Rock. Photo courtesy of Utah State Historical Society. C.R. Savage, photographer.

Old-time musicians of the Uintah Basin, LeRoy and Weltha Thacker. Photo courtesy of the Pattie Richards family collection.

Dancing to the Fiddle

THE DANCE MUSIC OF THE PIONEERS consisted largely of traditional tunes originally from Scotland and Ireland where it had accompanied the reels, jigs, and hornpipes that became the basis for the dances in the United States of America: the Virginia reels, quadrilles, etc. Towards the end of the pioneer period, round dancing became more and more acceptable and thus polkas, two-steps and waltzes in several variations found their way into pioneer dancing. These dances brought with them a different type of music, especially the waltz, whose smoothness and slower tempo contrasted sharply with earlier music with its lively tunes in either duple time (2/4 or 4/4) or triple time (6/8).

Although bands featuring wind instruments often played for dances in Nauvoo, on the plains as well as in Utah Territory, most Mormon dances depended on the fiddle, accompanied by whatever other instruments might be available, including the accordion, flute, guitar, reed organ, harmonica and banjo. The fiddle had a large repertoire of tunes, a clear carrying sound with droning which gave a semblance of harmony, and melodies punctuated with off-the-beat accents which gave the tunes a driving rhythm. The sound of a fiddle worked magic in the minds of those who loved to dance; the better the fiddler, the more profound the inspiration for dancing and its enjoyment. The power of the fiddle is illustrated by Mosiah Hancock in this story of his father, Levi, who was a fine fiddler:

In the lower level of her Provo home Merle Kartchner Shumway plays piano accompaniment to the violins of her son Larry and his children Nathan and Kirsten Shumway. Through their father and grandmother, Nathan and Kirsten learn the fiddle tunes made famous by their great-grandfather, Kenner C. Kartchner. Photo by Craig R. Miller, 1988.

While on a mission in Indiana, he stopped at a building where 400 people had gathered to dance. The man who was to furnish the music could not get his violin to work. Father's shoes were gone, and his pants were holey at the knees and behind, but he stepped up to the man and asked him what was the matter with his goose. Father took the thing and tuned it and made it fairly sing! The people danced until satisfied; then one of the men suggested that they get father a new suit, hat, and boots because he had fixed the violin and because they had had so much enjoyment. So they bought him a new suit, hat and boots! [32]

A fiddle is really a violin and the word "fiddle" is simply a very old name for the instrument. "Fiddling" is different from "violining" only in style, with "fiddling" referring specifically to a folk style of playing the violin that features droning on open strings, ornamented melodic lines and a pervasive off-beat accent. Although standard tuning for the violin is GDAE, in the fiddling world there are other tunings as well which help give fiddling its distinctive sonority. For example, in some tunes like "Rattlesnake" and "Bob-Tailed Mule," the lower two strings are raised a whole step from G and D to A and E (AEAE), which puts them an octave below the other two strings. This enlarges the sonority of the fiddle by increasing the ability for droning. The strings not being played vibrate sympathetically, reinforcing certain of the pitches played on the melody strings. This tuning also makes possible playing the music an octave lower which, with the sympathetic vibrations of the upper strings, brings a different tone color to the performance.

In "The Drunkard's Hiccups," a variant of this tuning lowers the high E to a C#, which tunes the strings into an A chord, AEAC#. Besides offering a variety of droning possibilities, it also allows the fiddler to drone on the lower string(s) while plucking the other strings with the little finger of the left hand.

Some fiddlers refer to these fiddle tunings as being in the Italian key, possibly from the technical musical term for non-standard tunings, *scordatura*. In any case, the enhanced resonance of the fiddle produced by such tunings gives fiddle music a unique sonority which evokes a distinct aesthetic response in listeners and dancers.

The piano came into general use towards the end of the pioneer period and because of its great tonal resources it became an important instrument for accompanying dancing. As pioneer communities moved into the twentieth century, the piano took on a greater role in playing the music, but most often the tunes were those of earlier times. Depending on several things including the ability of the performer, the role of the piano ranged from playing just straight chordal accompaniment for the fiddle to an enlarged role of playing along with the lead instruments and finally to being the prime if not sole instrument to play. A fine piano player's ability in playing the tunes surely added inspiration and exuberance to the dancing atmosphere.

This fiddle was given to LeRoy Thacker by his Mormon bishop in Altamont, Duchesne County. As a poignant reminder of the role the entire family played in perpetuating the musical heritage of the Uintah Basin, it now graces the wall above the fireplace of his daughter's home. Photo by Craig R. Miller, 1987.

Clockwise from top:

Salt Lake City's original Salt Palace was a grand exibition hall that was often used for dancing. Photo by C.R. Savage, courtesy Utah State Historical Society.

View of Orderville shortly after the turn of the twentieth century, when community dances were held in the Mormon ward situated in the center of town. Photo courtesy of Rena Tait.

Enterprise Orchestra. Photo by Hal Cannon, 1977.

The Story of Old-Time Mormon Dance

Settling Deseret

Much has been written about the Mormon migration to the valley of the Great Salt Lake during the middle of the nineteenth century. The culture that the pioneers introduced into the Great Basin region was primarily that of America's Northeast, augmented by traditions brought by converts from northwestern Europe. The pioneers brought with them a great respect for the arts and humanities and high ideals of education. Within a week of the arrival in the valley, they constructed a bowery where dances could be held, and among the first large buildings constructed were the Social Hall and the Salt Lake Theater where music, dance and fine dramas were presented.

It is not so widely known that Brigham Young, leader of The Church of Jesus Christ of Latter-day Saints (the Mormons) and governor of the Utah Territory, sent colonists from Salt Lake City to settle the farthest reaches of the Great Basin. Young sent pioneers north into Idaho, west to Nevada, and south to California and Arizona to populate the kingdom of God on earth, which the Mormons called Deseret. The pioneers of these settlements were carefully picked to ensure the successful growth of each well-organized and often self-sufficient new community. Providing an artistic outlet for the settlers of these communities remained a priority, for in addition to farmers, carpenters and a blacksmith, each village was sent an old-time fiddler. [33]

The landscape of the early Mormon West had its own distinct features: planned communities laid out in a grid pattern with uncommonly wide streets, long fencerows planted with Lombardy poplar trees, a complex system of irrigation ditches watering luxuriant green fields, and the distinctive Mormon hay derricks standing tall against a background of desert mountain peaks. In a very short time, rustic frontier cabins were replaced by elaborate Gothic Revival or Victorian cottages, often built by English or Scandinavian craftsmen of local stone. At the center of each village was a church which functioned as the social as well as the religious center of the community. Larger towns had a tabernacle for regional church gatherings and formal presentations or a social hall where concerts, theatrical presentations and dances took place. Many communities built one or more dance halls, private or civic.

To this day, remnants of this cultural landscape stand witness to the Mormon settlements of the nineteenth century throughout the Great Basin. The wide streets and sturdy houses remain even as the poplars die and the irrigated fields give way to subdivisions and superhighways. Though few nineteenth-century structures used for dancing still stand, a number of privately owned twentieth-century dance halls exist, some built as late as the 1940s. These structures are locally famous for their sprung wooden floors, their vernacular construction and decor, and the spectacular beauty of their environs. Built on the edge of precipices, by hidden lakes or canyon streams, a number of romantically named open-air dance halls provide enduring evidence of the ongoing importance of dance in Mormon communities of the West.

Monthly social dances at the Rulon C. Allred Building in Bluffdale still attract over a hundred dancers, but before its construction, the monthly dances called by Joseph Lymon Jessop and later by his son, Rosy, formed a social focus for their religious community. Photo courtesy of Rosy Jessop.

Built in 1853, the Isaac Chase Home in Salt Lake's Liberty Park is the home of the Utah Arts Council Folk Arts Program. The Chase Home Museum of Utah Folk Art exhibits the State Collection of Folk Art and it is the site of the annual August concert series, Mondays in the Park. Photo by Dave Stanley, 1988.

THE CHASE HOME

Dancing was very popular in the home of Isaac Chase, built in what is now Salt Lake City's Liberty Park during the years 1853-1854. Though it had eight rooms, it was not particularly large but it did have a large kitchen and living room with a wide fireplace and the Chases were very hospitable to people coming there for dancing parties. The house still stands today, and appropriately serves as the office and museum for the Folk Arts Program of the Utah Arts Council, which is dedicated to the preservation and perpetuation of traditional arts in the state. Brigham Young, who was Isaac's partner in the milling business, often came to visit, accompanied by his good friend and counselor, Heber C. Kimball:

> The floors had no carpet to be removed, nor any waxing to be done, and if the fiddlers came . . . there was [sure] to be a gathering of young folks. . . . President Young was not backward in taking the initiative, for he was fond of dancing. There would soon be a Cotillion, Money Musk, Sir Roger de Coverley, or a Schottische Reel. Bro. Brigham Young was a famous dancer, and certainly one of the most graceful pictures of all those popular men of the olden time. There were no restrictions about time, and it was often in the early morning hours, when the young people wended their way homeward.[34]

Larry Shumway

Building Community through Dance

THE FEW ARTICLES AND MASTER'S THESES that discuss the history of Mormon dance generally agree that Mormon dance parties had their own special atmosphere. In her thesis "Early Utah Dances," Laraine Miner discusses how Mormon culture developed its rich and distinctive style of social dance: "The religious tenents have provided an atmosphere for its flourishing, and have contributed a wholesome, joyous feeling to the style." She also contends, "The historical influence of persecution shaped the style at first by giving it a fervency bordering on defiance."[35]

Indeed, in the early, difficult years of the LDS Church's development in the Midwest, dances reinforced community identity. Later, on the trek across the plains and in the valleys of the Intermountain West, weary pioneers left the drudgery of building a new life in difficult surroundings for a few hours to come together and "make a joyful noise unto the Lord." They danced in celebration of their survival, despite occasional tensions with their neighbors and hard economic times.

According to journal accounts and newspaper reports, it mattered not whether pioneers danced on the prairie by the light of a campfire or whether Salt Lake City's social elite tripped "the light fantastic toe" to the gleam of crystal chandeliers. The simple truth is that early Mormons were a dancing people. In the early days, set dances in the form of quadrilles and Virginia reels were the dances of choice, for during an evening each individual interacted with nearly every other dancer on the floor.

In some respects, this early style of dance was a symbol of the social order required in Mormon society. Sets of dancers were arranged back to back and honeycombed row upon row like a living beehive, a proper representation of Mormon society. Before them stood one leader who masterfully called the sequence of perfectly matched dance figures, and in obedience to the call each man would reach for his partner's hand and lead her through the ephemeral maze. Error caused by any individual through inattention,

Seated in their Bluffdale home in Salt Lake County, Rosy Jessop laughs with his wife, Ellen, and their grandchildren about the monthly old-time dances he has called since the 1970s. Photo by Craig R. Miller, 1998.

defiance or simple misstep disrupted the order and jeopardized the successful completion of the dance and the enjoyment of the entire set of dancers. Indeed, the completion of the dance depended on each individual, just as the advancement of Mormon society depended on the cooperation and industriousness of each of its members.

The early pioneers had envisioned settlements that would bind together a new religious nation named Deseret. But the occupation of federal troops in the 1850s and the building of railways in the 1860s forever changed that dream, tying Utah and the Mormon settlements of the Great Basin to the greater destiny of the United States. It is no wonder that these changes of the nineteenth century disrupted established patterns of social order and behavior. As might be expected, this disruption was also reflected on the dance floor.

Brothers Christian and Peter Christensen directed the Box Elder Academy of Music and Dancing in Brigham City. Three of Christian's sons, Willam, Harold and Lew, studied at the academy and later became national figures in the world of professional ballet. This picture of the Brigham City Dance Hall was taken in 1908. Photo courtesy of Special Collections and Archives, Merrill Library, Utah State University.

First Family Orchestra of Gunlock, Washington County. Vernon, Gladys, Wallce and Lester. Photo courtesy of the Lynne Clark Historical Collection, St. George, Rose McAllister, donor.

The Round Dance Revolution

BY THE 1880s, THE SETTLEMENT LANDSCAPE of the Mormon West had stabilized. Friction between the LDS Church and the federal government diminished, political boundaries were secured, and Mormon dominance in population and economics made Salt Lake City the *de facto* capital of the Great Basin and the central Colorado River drainage. Through planning, cooperation and obedience, the desert bloomed as the proverbial rose. In thirty short years, the Mormon pioneers and their descendants converted large sections of arid landscape to bucolic pasture and farmland. Frail frontier outposts, now assured of their destiny, turned their attention to the outside world and to modern trends.

As Mormon communities matured and prospered, the function of community dance shifted. No longer did pioneers meet to reinforce identity and strengthen their resolve against a hostile physical and cultural environment. In these more gentle times, the community dance became a much-anticipated opportunity for boys and girls of the community to meet in a supervised atmosphere and a place where married couples could socialize and enrich their spirits. Community dances still provided a forum where the community collectively expressed cultural and religious values, but as the social needs of the community changed, so changed the dances themselves.

Davis Bitton's 1977 article, "These Licentious Days': Dancing Among the Mormons" focuses on the social tension caused by the introduction of round dancing in the late nineteenth century. Round dances differed from the old quadrilles and reels in that couples danced in a more intimate, closer position and often moved independently of other dancers about the floor. Bitton concludes that "The question of dancing among the Latter-day Saints is of no import theologically, but it is a good example of the inevitable stresses and strains in the interface between religion and popular culture."[36] Bitton's history, meticulously assembled from journals, newspaper accounts and archival holdings, thoughtfully tells the story of this controversy, which is still told in more fragmented form by today's living old-time dance musicians.

Although round dances such as the waltz and schottische were traditional expressions of Mormon immigrants from Germany and Scandinavia, the church leaders' Protestant-American sensibilities were offended by the public embrace suggested in the standard ballroom position. It was considered scandalous for a man to be seen in public with his arm around any woman, much less someone who was not his wife!

Members of the Wasatch Mountain Club enjoy a Saturday evening dance at the Hermitage, Ogden Canyon, March 31, 1923. Photo courtesy of University of Utah Marriott Library Special Collections, Wasatch Mountain Club Collection.

Despite the protestations and prohibitions of church leaders who preferred the older style of set dances, a preference for round dances took hold at the grassroots level and spread throughout the region. To some, the very choreography of the round dances threatened to erode the structure and social order of Mormon society. Scandalously embracing couples spinning dizzily in erratic patterns around the dance floor epitomized the anarchic chaos which nineteenth-century Mormon enlightenment was specifically designed to foil. Thus, the round-dance revolution in Utah was immediately perceived as a direct challenge to church authority

Saltair, built in 1893, was one of the grandest dance pavilions the world has ever known. Photo by Wilkes, courtesy of the Utah State Historical Society.

At first round dances were totally banned, but fearing young people would leave church dances for the uncontrolled private dance halls, church authorities eventually allowed round dances to slip into the repertoire. They first arrived in the form of the waltz quadrille, where during the usual figures of a dance set, one section would permit a few bars of music where couples could waltz together in the closed, ballroom position. A story that circulates in oral tradition recalls a general authority of the church who was seen by Brigham Young enjoying a waltz quadrille. In response to Young's admonitions, he admitted that he had indeed participated in the dance but was actually "quadrilling" more than he was waltzing.

A popular compromise was found in dances that had a promenade figure in 4/4 time followed by a short (or more expanded) waltz chorus. After very elegant promenades, bows and stiff Victorian poses, dances like the jewel, the Baltimore, the Chicago glide and le grace slipped almost unnoticed into 3/4 meter, inviting the dancers to slide into the seductive, sensuous waltz. Technically these dances were not waltzes, so they further danced around the prohibition and paved the way for a full acceptance of the waltz and round dancing in general. Eventually church decrees became so vague that local bishops could sometimes allow three round dances during an evening, then four, or eventually whatever was necessary to encourage the young people to return and dance where church supervision was available. [37]

By the turn of the century, round dances had supplanted nearly every other social dance form in Mormon communities. The rebellious generation which had introduced the scandalous waltz were now mature members of a well-established church and stable society. Unlike their pioneer ancestors, they did not dance defiantly to show their determination to overcome hard times, nor did they dance intent on building community cohesion. Secure in their bounty and certain of their future, this fortunate generation celebrated the hard-earned beauty and fullness of life in their social dancing.

Although floor managers still enforced the rule that "daylight" be visible between partners and escorted unruly elements outside, the round dances were now extolled for their grace, elegance and decorum. Ironically, the old quadrilles of the pioneers were sometimes considered too rowdy, no longer embodying the ideals of proper social dancing. [38]

The David Smith Orchestra, Salt Lake City, played at Saltair in 1906 and 1907. Mr. Smith, director and cellist, is third from left on the second row. His wife Pauline is in the front row, middle, holding her violin. Photo 1907, courtesy of the Lynne Clark Historical Collection, Polly Stirland, donor.

Saltair dancers, 1914. Photo courtesy of Utah State Historical Society.

SALTAIR

The queen of all dedicated places of entertainment was the Saltair resort on the shore of the Great Salt Lake. Built in 1893, well after the pioneer period, it represented the ultimate recreational resort for the citizens of Salt Lake City. In size and scope it had no peer in the United States at that time. The dancing pavilion was 140 x 250 feet with a roof supported by an iron framework that left no pillars or other obstructions on the floor. A railway brought hundreds of recreation-seekers daily to Saltair and activities continued into the night with the place being "lighted with 1,250 incandescent and forty arclights giving the place a fairylike appearance as they were reflected in the placid waters of the lake on a calm summer night." [39]

Larry Shumway

The Sam Chidester Orchestra plays for a dance in the Teasdale Cultural Hall, Wayne County. Photo courtesy of Lell Heaps.

Delta's fantastic Billy Van's Dance Hall was built in 1934 by the owner, Billy Van de Vanter. It was decorated with thousands of mirrored tiles and the dance ball suspended from the ceiling had a replica of the Salt Lake Mormon Temple on top. An electrical train circled the globe's equator and a small airplane pulled a sign saying "We dance next Saturday." The hall closed in 1960 and is being restored today. Photo courtesy of Utah State Historical Society.

The Golden Years of Mormon Dance

IN THE TWENTIETH CENTURY, COMMUNITY dances continued to be an inseparable part of the social fabric throughout the region. At ward dances, babies wrapped in quilts would sleep on benches lining the room as their siblings, parents and grandparents danced. In more rural areas dances were held in ranch houses where all the furniture would be carried outside to make room. Children were often laid to sleep on couches placed in the yard. Merle Shumway of Snowflake, Arizona remembers sleeping in a horse-drawn wagon parked in the shadows just beyond the lantern light that streamed through the windows. As she drifted off to sleep, she watched the silhouetted dancers spinning from room to room to the accompaniment of pump organ, guitar, mandolin and violin.

Stories abound regarding whole families who traveled all day by wagon and horseback to attend ranch dances. Such dances often began at around eight in the evening; at midnight everyone stopped for a big dinner, only to continue dancing from 2 AM until dawn. After a big breakfast, those who were short of sleep could catch up on the long wagon ride back home.

Until the outbreak of World War II, dances continued to be an integral part of everyday life and a vital part of life's more memorable moments. Virtually every holiday was an excuse to hold a community dance. Young people met and courted at the dances and then held dances to celebrate their weddings. Dances raised money to send young men off to serve missions for the church or to bid farewell to men leaving for military service. Later, dancing remained a featured event at church-sponsored Old Folks Days when spry elderly dancers participated as honored guests.

The Cosy Corner outdoor dance hall was situated on the south side of scenic Highway 24 near the Nielson Gust Mill. Cottonwood trees sprout though the foundation of the old bandstand and straw is stacked on the round concrete pad. Photo by Jerry Urlacher, 1999.

Clinton Peterson of Loa, Wayne County, has played in Peterson family bands for decades. Now he perpetuates the old-time traditions with the Poverty Bench Boys. Photo by Keith Jones, 1993.

A repertoire of dances ultimately developed in the Mormon West that reflected the cultural and geographic influences of the Mormons' first century as a community. That lasting repertoire identified not only a region but a people and a lifestyle. Many styles of dance passed through the region, were enjoyed for a period and were then forgotten—but not these. These struck a harmonious chord that resonated with other aspects of Mormon culture. These were the dances which families and communities chose to hold as their own, to remember for a lifetime and to hand down to grandchildren along with stories of pioneer ancestors, stories of faith, and simple stories of life and love. And these are the dances that still exist in rural and close-knit Utah communities in the second millennium.

Wayne County's old-time dance legacy survives in the music of the Poverty Bench Boys Band. Among its members are Clinton Peterson and Sam Chidester's grandson, Lell Heaps. Here the Poverty Bench Boys play for Capitol Reef National Park's Harvest Homecoming Celebration. Photo by Thea Nordling, 1998.

Origins of Old-Time Tunes and Dances

MULTIPLE THEORIES ABOUND REGARDING the origins of specific dances and melodies. Many communities now believe their ancestors invented a tune or a dance which has not been seen or heard anywhere else, and in some cases that certainly is true. More likely the dance or music was introduced to the community from the outside world long before the time to which current memories extend.

Of this old-time repertoire, many of the tunes and dances were brought to Utah by the pioneers. Many of these are mentioned in journal accounts including the Virginia reel--also known by its English name, Sir Roger de Coverly--and the spontaneously called square dances known as quadrilles.

Dance musician Merle Shumway claims the fiddle tune "Black Hills Waltz" was composed by Mormon pioneers and was inspired by the dark forested mountains of the Laramide Range, which the pioneers crossed on their way to Utah. Other tunes which have substantial claim to local composition include "The Rattlesnake," which is a fiddler's *tour de force* for the Kartchner/Shumway family, formerly of Snowflake, Arizona, and "The Clayhole Waltz," named for

Pete Hastings and Desie Reber dance in the Nature Center at Zion National Park during the 1988 Southern Utah Folklife Festival. Photo by Carol Edison, 1988.

a favored camping spot between the cane fields of Washington County and the Zion Canyon home of the musicians of the Gifford family.

Many other tunes and dances which the Mormon pioneers brought west were popular in the Northeast where the faith originated, but then, as the early Mormons traveled west and south to Ohio and eventually to Illinois and Missouri, they absorbed the culture of southern converts to the religion. Much of the Shumway family heritage, for example, can be traced to Mississippi and, indeed, much of the family musical repertoire is directly attributable to the southern branches of the family. Merle Shumway's father, legendary fiddler Kenner C. Kartchner, recorded his life in journals and meticulously notated the "origins" of the tunes he learned.[40] Much of his dance-music repertoire was collected during the years he worked as a ranch hand; the tunes he helped popularize in the Mormon settlements of Arizona were popular in ranching communities as far east as Texas and the southern Great Plains. Kartchner's experiences are a fine example of the sharing of traditions in frontier Mormon settlements, and the remnant references to "hoedowns" and "breakdowns" in the names of tunes are strong indications that there was a southern component to the old-time repertoire.

The Gifford family of Zion Canyon has kept the rich music traditions of Southern Utah alive for generations. They play tunes like "Haste to the Wedding" which is hundreds of years old, and they play their own family's compositions like "The Clayhole Waltz." For years they were called "The Pitchfork Band" because of their signature rhythm instrument, a pitchfork, played here by Lulabelle Seegmiller. Photo by Carol Edison, 1978.

The Virgin River Valley in Zion Canyon was home to generations of Crawford and Gifford family musicians in the villages of Springdale and Rockville. Photo by Craig R. Miller, 1998.

Along with the Texas path of music is the hint of a Mexican connection. Anglo pioneer communities in the Southwest settled on lands previously occupied by the Spanish settlements of colonial Mexico, and the aspects of Spanish culture that flowed north from Mexico City were shared with Anglo settlements in the American Southwest. Most notable is the example of the tune and dance known variously as "Put Your Little Foot," "Have You Seen My New Shoes?" "The 'Souviann," "The Varsouvienne," or its name in Spanish, *"La varsoviana."* In Spanish the word *"varsoviana"* refers to something or someone from Warsaw, Poland, or *"Varsovia."*

In the 1860s when Emperor Maximilian came to power in Mexico, he brought the culture of European court life to the New World. Dance forms including the waltz, the schottische, the polka, the Polish mazurka and the variation known as *"La varsoviana"* surged in popularity on both sides of the Rio Grande.¹¹ Indeed, old-time dances like the *vals, chotis, polka, mazurka-polka, and la varsoviana* are still popular among descendants of colonial New Mexicans in Utah and across the entire region. It seems likely, then, that the varsouvienne found its way to Utah from Mexico.

Utah has a curious connection to Mexican culture which continues even to the present day. When the church manifesto banning polygamy was announced in the 1890s prior to statehood, many polygamous families fled across the border and established Mormon "colonies" in northern Mexico. Over the years, many have returned to Utah, but family ties remain strong with relatives remaining in Mexico. Descendants of those Mexican colonists regularly gather for reunions in Utah where they socialize and pass the family history and heritage along to the next generation. The Shirley Clark family, formerly of Colonia Dublan, has retained much of their Mexican music heritage and they have passed it down in the family setting long after their return to Utah.

A native of Colonia Dublan, Mexico, J. Shirley Clark was born into a musical family in 1904. After the family moved to Logan, Utah, Mr. Clark formed his own family band that was known for their Mexican music and novelty songs. Mr. and Mrs. Clark pose among Mexican sombreros, marimbas and guitars in their Logan living room. Photo by Craig Miller, 1987.

Spanish references in the Mormon dance repertoire are obvious when they occur in dance names such as "The Spanish Waltz," but often they are hidden in the melody of a dance tune, as in the varsouvienne-like pattern introduced by the opening glissandos of "The Black Hawk Waltz." The Mexican origin of "Over the Waves" is indisputable, for it was composed in 1888 by Juventino Rosas, an Otomi Indian from Guanajuato, Mexico. *"Sobre las olas,"* as it is known in Spanish, was, worldwide, the second most popular tune of the nineteenth century, second only to "The Blue Danube Waltz." [42] To this day, Utahns descended from Spanish-speaking New Mexicans play *"Sobre las olas,"* but it is still debatable whether the tune entered the Mormon dance repertoire directly from Mexico or whether it was a part of the great wave of nineteenth-century ballroom dances which swept west with the tide of East Coast American culture.

Completion of the transcontinental railroad at Promontory Summit, Utah in 1869 forever tied the cultural destiny of the Mormon settlements in the West to the manifest destiny of American popular culture. Scores of ballroom dances passed through Utah in the latter half of the nineteenth century, but the majority of the ones kept in the repertoire were in the form of two-part dances consisting of an introductory promenade in 4/4 meter followed by a waltz section in three-quarter time.

Given the reluctance of LDS Church officials to permit the controversial waltz, perhaps these two-part dances, which were technically not waltzes, were a popular compromise at the time. The jewel, the Baltimore, the Chicago

Seated at her home piano at the age of 98, Vida Adams Rouche still played the old-time dance music that was popular when she was pianist for the Adams Family Band of Layton, Davis County. Photo by Keith Jones, 1995.

glide, and le grace are all products of that era. Their names make no mention of the waltz figures they contain hidden behind a series of walking figures, bows and poses. Even the old Scottish folk song "Coming through the Rye" inspired a popular ballroom dance, but the ambiguity of its path to Utah raises the question of whether it was just a fad of the times or whether it was first danced by Scottish immigrants to Utah as a poignant reminder of the homeland they left behind.

Many tunes and dances did come from the British Isles, Scandinavia and Germany along with European converts to the LDS church. Round dances like the waltz and schottische (called *schotis* in Sweden or *Reinlander* in Norway and other parts of the Continent) entered the European folk repertoire generations earlier, long before migration to Utah. Today it is impossible to know if some tunes and dances entered Utah originally from Europe, Mexico or the East Coast.

The European big circle and "family-style" waltzes (as they are known in Swedish) differ from the American ballroom waltzes of the nineteenth century in that couples close their waltz step on count two while executing small clockwise turns within a larger circle of couples progressing counter-clockwise around the dance floor. In its free form, this style of waltz produces a uniform circulation of whirling couples turning about the room.

This European style of waltz is also found in big-circle formations like the Oslo waltz, in which dancers execute a series of synchronized steps that often result in a change of partners before closing with a short pattern of small clockwise couple turns.

Just as the waltz ignited tirades before the turn of the twentieth century, it still sparks arguments on Utah's turn-of-the-twenty-first-century dance floors. But now it is because the beloved waltz is danced differently in different parts of the state. Areas in Utah with a strong Scandinavian heritage tend to favor the European waltz step, but elsewhere practitioners of the standard American ballroom waltz or "box-step waltz" take two walking steps and bring their feet together on count three rather than two. They denounce the European style as nothing similar to their waltz at all and sometimes call it "The Two-Step Waltz" or even "The Ignoramus Waltz."

According to Lloyd Shaw, champion of the old-time American dance revival of the mid-twentieth century, the standard American ballroom waltz was a mid-nineteenth-century invention that grew out of the Polish *redowa*, a dance of the mazurka family which is also executed in 3/4 time.[43] After decades of dance instruction when he aggressively tried to eliminate the European folk waltz from western dance floors, he very grudgingly admitted, "The two-step waltz is several generations older than the standard waltz of today. I knew it, but I tried to shut my eyes to it. However, now that I have been living with the history of the dance, I simply must admit that it has a longer lineage, a longer story than the waltz I love."[44] So strong is the love felt for the waltz that even dance scholars betray their own reputations out of loyalty to the dance!

Postcard featuring the Dancing Pavilion at Lagoon Resort in Davis County. Photo courtesy of the Utah State Historical Society.

Dancers at the Hurricane Senior Center enjoy a "Circle-All." Photo by Craig R. Miller, 1989.

Utahns who are staunch believers in one form of the waltz generally decry the other version as "just plain wrong," when in actuality they indeed are completely different dances. Although they are danced to the same 3/4 meter and share the name "waltz," they have separate origins, steps and formations. Consequently, while each waltz form is enjoyed in complete satisfaction by its respective practitioners, problems occur when both versions appear simultaneously on the same dance floor. Couples on differing trajectories may crash into each other and mixed couples wrestle over whether to turn clockwise or counter-clockwise and whether to close their footwork on count two or count three. In contrast to the whirling European waltz, the American ballroom waltz inspires a hypnotic glide as couples move independently across the floor in straight lines or in wide, curving sweeps, dips and turns. And the box step leads dancers to turn counter-clockwise, exactly opposite to the turns of the European waltz.

The old-time schottische also exists in several distinct forms in Utah. The standard European schottische with a forward traveling pattern followed by couple turns is favored in some communities, but it has several outgrowths which are decidedly American. Using the same music, couples can dance the heel-and-toe schottische holding hands in a "horseshoe" position, without European-style couple turns. Or they can dance a two-couple "horse and buggy" version or the "double schottische," which is a unique trio version danced by one man and two women that earned the local name " the old polygamy schottische."

Although there is reasoned debate about whether a novelty dance like the patty-cake polka was introduced by inter-national folkdance instructors in the twentieth century, the dance does have its Danish counterparts. Similarly, the couple dance to "Pop Goes the Weasel" may have been a twentieth-century invention, but its use in community dances fits the old-time function and there is no dispute that it is an ancient song known by Utah's English-speaking immigrants. In fact, a great number of tunes like "Blow Ever across the Wild Moor," "Haste to the Wedding," and other fiddle tunes and reels which accompanied the old quadrilles can be traced directly to the British Isles.

Other dances like "Danish slide-off" are specifically mentioned in early Utah reminiscences or journals, implying introduction by foreign pioneers. And dances like the finger polka, heel-toe polka, and seven-step schottische all have direct ties to European folk dances on the Continent.

Using Roger Lax and Frederick Smith's *The Great Song Thesaurus*, it is easy to identify the origin of many tunes which are staples in Utah's old-time dance repertoire because they were well-known compositions in their own day. "Over the Ocean Deep," as it is known on Utah dance floors, was composed in 1838 by Henry Russell, but its offi-

Pianist Mabel Allred first learned the old-time dance repertoire from fiddler Ianthus Barlow when she was a teenager in Colorado City. For many years she accompanied social dances for her church group in Bluffdale, Salt Lake County. Photo by Craig R. Miller, 1996.

cial name is "A Life on the Ocean Wave." In 1889 this famous tune was made the official march of the Royal Marines.[45] Another internationally famous tune, "The Skaters Waltz," was composed by Emil Waldteufel in 1882.[46] And it might be described as inevitable that Victorian dance masters choreographed other nineteenth-century hit tunes like "Narcissus," composed by Ethelbert Nevin in 1891, and "Darling Nelly Grey," which was composed by

Benjamin Russell Hanby in 1856. [47]

The origins of other dance tunes are obscured by time. For example, Quentin Nisson of Washington, Utah, plays a solo piano tune of late-nineteenth-century style that he calls a "Jim Booth Waltz." It is one of a number of tunes his father Edward learned from professional photographer and fiddler Jim Booth, who lived in southwest Utah's Dixie around the turn of the century. Whether Booth composed these tunes or learned them from some other source does not change the fact that these are now a part of the Dixie heritage, named for a local musician who obviously had a lasting influence on his community.

A dance or song which belongs to a community's heritage may have traveled a very circuitous route before finding its adopted home in Utah. A good example is "The Home Waltz," one of the best-known dance tunes that closed almost every old-time dance in Utah. Whereas the old-time dancers often competed to fill their dance cards with the maximum number of different partners, at the end of the evening "The Home Waltz" was a gentle reminder for dancers to find their original escorts and return to the comfort of home together.

The tune for "The Home Waltz" began life as "Sicilian Air," arranged by an Englishman, Sir Henry Rowley Bishop. It gained the lyrics of "Home Sweet Home" in 1823, thanks to John Howard Payne, and won international fame as the encore song for the nineteenth-century Swedish soprano Jenny Lind. [48] In the period when social dance was the most popular form of recreation in the West, "The Home Waltz" found its own sweet home in the hearts of Utahns.

Indeed, the practice of borrowing a piece of music or a dance and eventually taking ownership of it continued well into the twentieth century. "Redwing," a nationally popular song published in 1907 by Kerry Mills with words by Thurland Chattaway, [49] is Utah's most frequently played tune to accompany a circle two-step. Mills borrowed the catchy tune from Robert Schumann's "Happy Farmer" or "Frölicher Landmann," published in 1848. Similarly, what the Thacker family of the Uintah Basin calls "The Big Foot Taylor Waltz" is better known as "Cattle Call," composed by Tex Owens in 1934. [50] Its colorful local name derives from frequent requests for the tune by a regular dancer, Mr. Taylor, who evidently had very large feet! Once the Thacker family abandoned the original title and applied the new one, the adoption process was complete and "The Big Foot Taylor Waltz" belonged to the entire community.

The "Circle All" as it is performed in Utah's Dixie is a striking example of how modern music can be incorporated into the existing repertoire and how a traditional dance can be adapted to enhance its original community function. "Circle All" begins with a figure found in the standard circle two-step. A circle of women holding hands surrounds a circle of men, and both groups circulate in opposite directions to the accompaniment of a favorite old-time tune. When the music stops, each man turns to dance with the closest woman as the band changes the dance form from a march to a waltz, a schottische, or perhaps a more contemporary form like the Charleston, swing or fox-trot. As the music changes back to the march, partners separate and reform their circles to repeat the sequence and find a new partner. This "new" old-time dance is performed in Utah's Dixie, a popular retirement area where regular weekly dances attract a higher ratio of women than men. This dance allows everyone to get on the floor, with or without a partner, and because of the multiple partner changes, even shy single ladies of old-style etiquette are spared the embarrassment of asking a gentleman to dance.

The Starlight outdoor dance hall, Toquerville. Photo by Hal Cannon, 1977.

Best-friend cousins Verna Black (left) and Maryette Carling have played for community dances in Colorado City for decades. Even today, monthly dances in Colorado City attract hundreds of people and the old-time dances still form the bulk of the repertoire. Photo by Craig R. Miller, 1993.

The Old-Time Dance Repertoire in Contemporary Times

AT THE TURN OF THE TWENTY-FIRST CENTURY, old-time music is still found in Mormon communities from Grouse Creek in the northwest corner of Utah to Snowflake, Arizona, in the southeast part of the region. Yet among a dozen surveyed communities, considerable regional variation exists due to geographic distance, cultural differences and the personal styling, creativity, improvisation and preferences of significant local individuals.

The Long Valley communities of Orderville and Alton, situated in a high river valley in southern Utah, are separated by only thirty miles from the cluster of towns that make up Utah's Dixie in the southwestern corner of the state. But those thirty miles include the canyons of Zion National Park, so even to this day the rugged terrain discourages much direct contact. As a result, the schottische and several other dances are danced differently and to different music in these communities. Members of the Orderville Orchestra still ask "How does that 'Dixie' schottische go?" and then can't get it right because they are so used to their own version.

Of all the towns surveyed, no two have retained exactly the same repertoire. The quadrille, Virginia reel, varsouvienne, waltz and schottische were probably found every-

Aleath Gifford plays drums with her own family band and with the Quentin Nisson band in Utah's Dixie. Photo by Craig R. Miller, 1989.

where until very recently, but some more obscure dances share surprising distribution patterns. The Chicago glide, for example, is a waltz form that was known by dancers in the Uintah Basin in the northeastern corner of the region, by community dancers in Bluffdale near Salt Lake City, and by dancers from the Mormon communities around the towns of Snowflake and Colorado City, Arizona, in the southernmost part of the region. It seems to have disappeared within the 300-mile stretch of communities situated in between. In fact, Merle Shumway, an octogenarian originally from Snowflake, thought it should be renamed the Arizona glide because she had never heard of it being done anywhere else.

That example is not unusual. Perhaps the best explanation for the selective amnesia of the full dance repertoire is that a dance was probably retained in a community because a particular individual liked it, played it, or requested it, thereby assuring it remained in the local repertoire. Evidence of this process is found in the many tunes named for specific individuals. Two examples are "Sam Chidester's Schottische," named for the old-time band leader in Wayne County near Capitol Reef National Park, and "Big Foot Taylor Waltz" from the Uintah Basin.

Another characteristic throughout the region is that the old-time dances that survived are the ones that had the best learning-to-enjoyment ratio. If a farming or ranching family only came to town once or twice a season, it stands to reason that they would not have been as adept at dancing as their urban, eastern counterparts. They may have had to relearn each dance on every occasion, so consequently the dances which were best-loved and best-remembered through several generations were likely the ones that were simple but satisfying because of their elegance or because they were just plain fun.

Many dances did not even need to be taught, and footwork could be as simple as just walking, but the real enjoyment of the dance came through the spontaneity of the called figures. There were a variety of unnamed walking dances with figures executed in a big circle, in longways sets like the Virginia reel, or in sets of four couples, the quadrilles, the much simpler ancestors of the modern square dance which developed in the mid-twentieth century.

Some dances achieve simplicity through sheer repetition, like the seven-step schottische, known in Western Europe from Scandinavia to Slovenia. In Hooper, in northern Utah, they know the dance by the name of the song they sing to it: "Wake Up, Jacob, Daddy Shot a Bear." Its seemingly complicated sequence mixes step counts of seven and three, with step-hops in four. During a dance, the musicians repeat the tune over and over until the dancers memorize the pattern. At that point conversation between partners becomes possible, adding an abiding interest to the dance that endures long after the glow of physical accomplishment wears off.

Perhaps more importantly, many of the old-time dances are couple mixers in which dancers follow a progression where partners are exchanged after one or more executions of the dance pattern. In any century, this provides another way to enliven a rather simple dance and to encourage everyone on the dance floor to become acquainted.

Following a turn-of-the-century tradition, on the morning of July fourth, Quentin Nisson's band serenades the town of Washington from the bed of a flatbed trailer. Photo courtesy of Quentin Nisson.

Orderville Orchestra rehearsing in the Orderville Senior Center: Allan and Twila Cox, harmonica; Reva Anderson, melodica; Rena Tait, piano; Norma Penny and Ruby Esplin, violin; Bernard Tait, bass guitar; Myrna Cox, spoons; Val Tait, guitar. Photo by Craig R. Miller, 1989.

Orderville: The Evolution of Dance in One Small Town

SITUATED AT THE BASE OF THE CARMEL CLIFFS in Kane County's beautiful Long Valley, Orderville was named for the United Order, the LDS Church-sponsored program in the nineteenth century that promoted communal living and self-sufficiency. Perhaps because of its isolation or the industriousness of its members, the Order lasted longer in Orderville than practically anywhere else. And indeed, life was complete in this small community that prided itself on producing everything it needed—including its own entertainment.

Founding pianist of the Orderville Orchestra, Mercy Blackburn Chamberlain (center), is pictured with two girlfriends. Photo courtesy of Rena Tait.

"Southern Utah: A Scenic Song" with words and music by Orderville's Howard Spencer, was published with an international copyright in 1923.

Shortly after the turn of the twentieth century, violinist Howard Spencer joined with pianist Mercy Chamberlain to found the first Orderville Orchestra. Howard was the high-school music teacher and a published composer. In those days most of the dancing was held in the versatile old ward hall, which was also the town's meeting center and the site for fine dramatic productions. Once all the pews and chairs were pushed to the walls, the sturdy wooden floor was perfect for dancing.

Community dancing in Orderville exemplifies the classic pattern throughout the Great Basin. At first, dances were held only in church buildings like the old ward hall and couples enjoyed the old-time dances exclusively, but in the nineteen thirties and forties, dancing moved into more public arenas such as the high-school gymnasium where the new fox-trot and swing dances joined the old quadrilles and round dances.

A few miles north along Highway 89, an outdoor dance hall at Hidden Lake featured weekend dancing and attracted couples traveling by automobile from all the surrounding communities. It was a location of uncommon

Founding violinist of the Orderville Orchestra, Howard Spencer was the high school music teacher and a published composer. Photo courtesy of Rena Tait.

Rena Tait discusses the history of old-time dance in Orderville. Photo by Craig R. Miller, 1989.

ORDERVILLE'S HERITAGE IN MUSIC AND STORIES

As Rena Tait tells the story of dancing in her hometown of Orderville, she recalls her own experiences as a dance musician. She pulls a page of photographs from her family album and points to a picture of Orderville pioneers, explaining it was taken in the old chapel where her mother played piano and where many of Rena's thirty-two aunts and uncles used to dance. Each face in the old photographs reminds her of a poignant life story or an incident that had a lasting impact on the community.

One of the most often-told stories about the United Order features a community dance where local history was made. Here is Rena's version: "In the days of the United Order all the boys had the same kind of pants. They were cut on the same pattern and all made exactly alike. This one enterprising young man decided he wanted something different so he saved some wool off a sheep he helped shear and when they went to Marysvale to sell the wool, he bought a pair of store pants. At the next dance they had, here he came out on the floor in those new store pants and everyone had eyes for him! This created quite a problem for the town because all the boys wanted fancy ones like he had. So the elders of the United Order got together and decided they would take his pants and cut them up for a pattern and use it in the clothing factory where they made their clothes and they made all the boys a pair like his store-bought pants."

That story found its way into this verse that Rena sings to the dance tune "Irish Washer Woman": "Oh, Johnny Carlin had no britches to wear / so he got him a sheepskin and made him a pair / with the skinny side out and the wooly side in! / Now what do you think of our Johnny Carlin?"

Craig R. Miller

Rena Tait's grandfather, Thomas Chamberlain, poses for a photograph with his eighteen sons, including Hans, husband of Mercy Chamberlain, founder of the Orderville Orchestra. Photo courtesy of Rena Tait.

beauty on a bench overlooking Long Valley. People still talk about the dance platform that extended over the lake, the string of lights leading along the shore to the concession stand, and the romantic spots sequestered in the shadows of the pines and willows. And they still laugh about the occasional tipsy dancer who splashed into the lake after a staggered misstep.

Throughout its history, the Orderville Orchestra has remained truly a community orchestra with an unbroken continuity of tradition. Many of the musicians have played for decades with overlapping tenures. Mercy Chamberlain, for example, was the main pianist over the years and it wasn't until the 1970s that her daughter, Rena Tait, took the lead.

Today the Orderville Orchestra still plays for the annual Hunters' Ball in autumn and serenades the town from the bed of a flatbed trailer on July 24, Pioneer Day. It also plays for special events like the Kane County Fair and for get-togethers in all the communities of Long Valley as far away as Alton. But the orchestra can most often be heard at the Orderville Senior Citizen Center, a reflection of the age of its members and its primary audience.

Photograph of the Orderville Orchestra playing for a community dance in the Valley High School gymnasium in the late 1940's. Charles Hepworth, mandolin; Ammron Humphries, guitar; Binnie Sorensen, harmonica; Berneta Tait, piano; Lyn Tait, mandolin. Photo courtesy of Rena Tait.

Thomas Chamberlain poses for a photograph with his fifteen daughters, sisters-in-law of Mercy Chamberlain, founder of the Orderville Orchestra. Photo courtesy of Rena Tait.

Tex Parker and His Wasatch Buckaroos play for a New Year's Eve dance at the Lazy Bar Ranch in Salt Lake County, 1947. Photo courtesy of Ralph and Faye Parker.

Twentieth-Century Technologies

During the early part of the twentieth century, radio and phonograph recordings ushered in a new period of music and dance. Just as in previous periods, nationally popular styles entered the region. Today's old-time musicians routinely recount stories of how they trained themselves to memorize tunes from late-night radio programs broadcast from as far away as Los Angeles and Tijuana. For the first time in history, musicians who played by ear could purchase a phonograph record and play a tune over and over again to copy every nuance of the original performance.

As a result, new styles of music and dance were introduced into the existing structure of local dances and sometimes added to the repertoire. Although many dances like the cakewalk and the Charleston entered the region as fads and then passed on, the fox-trot, one-step, and swing are twentieth-century dance styles which coexisted with the old-time repertoire and eventually became more popular. These were the dances which fit with the fantastically popular

This homemade recording from the mid 1940s featured music of Tex Parker and His Wasatch Buckaroos. Photo by Craig R. Miller, 1990.

music of the big band era and coincided with the boom in private dance-hall construction.

While Orderville's Rena Tait was growing up, the music of her generation included the remnants of Dixieland jazz, ragtime and the music of the big bands. Even now, when she plays the old-time tunes handed down from her parents' generation, Rena adds the lilt and syncopation which characterized the popular music of her own younger years. And to this day, senior citizens' dances in Utah's Dixie include a "Circle All" which uses the structure of the old-time circle two-step as a mechanism to include the more modern fox-trot and swing dance.

Although modern twentieth-century technology ushered in changes that may have jeopardized this dance-music tradition, it also can be credited for preserving a few treasured samples of old-time music. It is a marvel that so many good home recordings from the early part of the twentieth century exist today. Early recording devices included home-recording gramophones which cut grooves into soft wax discs and wire recordings that employed fragile wire filaments. Among the earliest are over two dozen tunes featuring Kenner C. Kartchner on violin and his daughter Merle K. Shumway on piano, recorded in 1943.

But it was the introduction of one-quarter-inch reel-to-reel recording tape and, later, cassette tapes that made home recordings convenient, portable and affordable. Across the region, from the early 1940s right up to the present day, families with foresight used these amateur recording devices to make home recordings and document their heritage in the form of family histories, stories and music. In the late 1950s and early 1960s, members of the Uintah Basin's Thacker family began recording family reunions, sing-alongs, letters sent to each other, and tributes in church and at funerals. Some of their most treasured recordings include Leroy and Weltha Thacker playing old-time dance tunes on violin and piano. Also in the early 1960s, a recording was made of Sam Chidester, beloved bandleader from Wayne County. Sam's band had been invited to play at a fiftieth wedding anniversary for dear friends who had moved to the Uintah Basin, but due to his advanced years, he could not make the long trip. Instead, he recorded their most requested tunes on cassette tape so the old-time dance could still take place.

Home recordings from the 1970s of Iron County's Enoch Orchestra and Orderville's Tait Family Band show how the repertoire of these community musicians evolved over time, gradually incorporating modern popular music like rock and roll, show tunes and country music into the old-time repertoire of dances.

Another extraordinary recording exists of the 1957 Centennial Pageant of Washington City in southwestern Utah. In addition to the locally written dramatization of the community's history presented by descendants of the town's founders, the presentation included songs, poetic recitations, and a re-creation of old-time social dancing to the accompaniment of the old Washington Orchestra. In the background, under the taped music, one can hear the footstep ghosts of dancers sliding across a platform stage, executing the Chicago glide and the all-but-forgotten Manitou. There is no way of knowing how many other old-time bands made recordings informally at home or in community settings, but finding those near-forgotten relics in attics, basements or storage closets is detective work that depends as much on luck and timing as persistence.

Scrapbook memorabilia of Tex Parker and His Wasatch Buckaroos. Photo by Craig R. Miller, 1990.

Tex Parker and His Wasatch Buckaroos play western swing music on Salt Lake's first television station, KDYL, 1949. Bruce Timothy, accordion; Tex Parker, violin; Alice Bangerter, vocals; Zane Parker, bass; Dick Tennant, guitar. Photo courtesy of Ralph and Faye Parker.

Old Rock Church, Cedar City. Photo by Craig R. Miller, 1995.

SAGEBRUSH FLANIGAN AND THE JOHN PERRY ORCHESTRA

In 1944, before Ellsworth "Sagebrush" Flanigan left to serve in the Navy in World War II, he asked local radio station KSUB to record the John Perry Orchestra that regularly played for KSUB Barn Dances at the Old Rock Church in Cedar City. Sagebrush especially loved the old-style dances and he planned to take the recordings with him on board ship as nostalgic mementos of the life he left behind. He also took a few branches of sagebrush, whose scent reminded him of his desert mountain home. As a result he was called "Sagebrush," a nickname which lasted. The recording of the band was made in the home of orchestra pianist Beth Leigh, formerly of Kanab, while four couples danced in their stocking feet to assure the band played with the correct speed and rhythm for dancing.

Sagebrush, when interviewed in his 80s, said John Perry and his orchestra members were old then! He also chuckled to admit he naively expected to find a phonograph player aboard ship during the war. He never even got to hear those recordings until after he returned home!

Today this recording provides a rare opportunity to hear the virtuosity and enthusiasm of local musicians born in the nineteenth century. Frozen in time, it takes us back to that afternoon in Beth Leigh's living room when a community of musicians and dancers came together to provide a sendoff for a young man going to war.

Because it was recorded to the accompaniment of actual dancers, we know the tempos, rhythms and phrasing are all correct, not imagined in the vacuum of a studio devoid of a critical dancing audience. Nor were these dance tunes remembered by musicians distanced by years from the height of their performing abilities. These musicians were in the most active years of their performing careers. The lilt and subtle emphasis they add to the upbeat in their varsouvienne and Spanish waltz are lost to most contemporary bands. And in addition to their virtuosity, their instrumental ornamentation, aesthetic style and choice of arrangements exhibit the straightforward clarity and drive that were so reflective of the region and its culture at that time.

Utah's Dance Halls

Although nationally popular bands could be heard by radio and phonograph across the region as far back as the 1920s, it was not until the 1930s that faster automobiles and paved highways made it possible for dancers to travel fifty miles or more to attend a dance and return home the same evening. This allowed dancing to shift from the almost exclusive province of local church sponsorship to privately owned dance halls that offered regular weekly dancing to live music.

Utah County, in particular, was known for its many fine dance halls. Several halls built in the middle of towns featured indoor dancing from October to May. But during the warm months, operations moved to outdoor dance halls situated around Utah Lake.

Pioneer Utahns had a strong tradition and intense love of dancing out of doors that was passed along to their descendants. Based on the example of the Salt Lake settlers, the first gatherings of each pioneer company were held under quickly constructed open-air boweries that were used until more solid structures could be built. The image of dances held in the open air finds its way into much

Pioneers on the Hole-in-the-Rock Trail held dances in the natural rock amphitheater known forever after as Dance Hall Rock. Photo by Craig Sorensen, 1996.

Mormon-based literature, and the legendary story of Dance Hall Rock along the Hole-in-the-Rock Trail in southern Utah, is one of the lasting narratives of Mormon courage and determination in the face of seemingly insurmountable odds. In 1879, over 200 people with 83 wagons were called to leave the town of Escalante and settle an isolated area of southeast Utah. They traversed 290 miles of desert and canyon country at an average of only 1.7 miles per day. On the final stretch, they had to lower their wagons and supplies down a 2,000-foot cliff to the Colorado River through a crevice carved in solid rock.

The pioneers camped along the trail near a large sandstone amphitheater with a solid rock floor suitable for dancing. To the accompaniment of the fiddle, the pioneers danced in the face of their hardships and made the impressive natural formation forever legendary as the original Dance Hall Rock.

The Purple Haze dance hall in Kingston, Piute County, has a dance floor of pink concrete. The structure is still used for family reunions and although the dance floor has been repaired in recent years, the patchwork has not been tinted in pink. This view is from the dance hall's picnic area, next to the rushing mountain stream, Kingston Creek. Photo by Craig R. Miller, 1995.

In celebration of Utah's centennial of statehood in 1996, a dance was held at Dance Hall Rock along the Hole-in-the-Rock Trail. Photo by Craig Sorensen, 1996.

The construction of open-air dance halls throughout the region during the 1930s is perhaps the best marker of Utah's golden age of social dance. Built for the sheer love of dance, these halls reveal the genius and imagination of those who dreamed of an idyllic spot where music, dance and the natural environment could combine to enhance the life of the common person.

Typically situated at the foot of towering canyon walls, by the waters of a cascading mountain stream, or near a calm irrigation ditch lined with whispering cottonwood trees, these outdoor dance halls sported romantic names like "The Rendezvous," "The Purple Haze," and "The Starlight." Here, to the accompaniment of big-band music, a whole generation of Utahns danced the fox-trot and swing, falling in love under the western sky.

In the Salt Lake Valley, dancers from as far away as Bingham Canyon would drive to Midvale to dance at a place nicknamed the Rooftop Gardens, which in actuality was the flat roof of a Mormon church. Income from the popular weekly dances funded the completion of the chapel on the building's main floor. In western Utah during World War II, flight crews in Wendover worked on the famed *Enola Gay* while servicemen danced with local residents in Jukebox Cave, a natural formation with a poured concrete floor tucked inside a mountain on the edge of the Bonneville Salt Flats.

Perhaps Utah's most dramatic dance location is the old dance hall at Palisade State Park in Sanpete County. Crowning a narrow ridge, the dance floor squeezed between the shore of Palisade Reservoir and a precipice which dropped hundreds of feet to the distant valley floor. Although time and neglect have nearly obliterated all physi-

Located on a knife-blade ridge between the lake and a precipice that drops several hundred feet to the valley floor, a cracked concrete floor is all that remains of the outdoor dance hall at Sanpete County's Palisade Lake. Photo by Craig R. Miller, 1998.

cal evidence of the dance hall, behind a berm of sagebrush and barbed wire the cracked remnants of the old concrete pad still edge precipitously close to the cliffside view into infinity. Anyone who ever danced here is still resplendent with memories of the romantic evenings at Palisade. One story explained that before evening dances began, several men would pull bales of native grasses across the concrete to prepare the hard surface so leather-soled shoes could glide across the floor properly. Domestically cultivated hay or straw did not serve the purpose. Sanpete native Afton Greaves remembers that after dancing late into the night the band sometimes serenaded the departing dancers from a barge in the lake.

Though not specifically a product of Mormon culture, the privately owned community dance hall also provided a much-needed community service. It was often a meeting place where Mormons could socialize with their "gentile," or non-Mormon, neighbors. Though often the dance hall helped bridge that cultural gap, it might also underscore differences. There are a few stories about instances when a local bishop was intent on closing down a private hall by organizing competing church-sponsored dances on the same evenings. But if one dance hall closed, another would open, and this continued across the region throughout the golden age of dance in Utah.

The S.S. Showboat sailed the waters of Utah Lake as the State's most unusual dance floor. Photo courtesy of Robert Carter.

The Future of Old-Time Dance

THE DANCE REPERTOIRE, MUSIC and associated social customs of the Mormon West are an important part of the region's cultural landscape. Though not as visible as the distinctive Mormon hay derrick in rural areas nor as obvious as the grid-like street layout of Mormon towns and cities, the cultural importance of the old-time dance traditions cannot be overlooked.

At the close of the twentieth century, it seems that popularly accepted symbols of contemporary American "country" culture have begun to obscure our regionally distinct heritage of music and dance. When asked to describe the music and dance of the Mormon West, the average Utahn is likely to conjure up silver-screen images from Hollywood westerns, lightning-fast fiddle tunes from bluegrass or fiddle contests, or cadres of uniformly fringed and petticoated dancers executing a precision clogging routine. Unfortunately, each time we perpetuate these ideas and defer to the images and sounds circulated by the mass media, we contribute to the demise of a once-vibrant regional tradition of community music and dance. Perhaps the best explanation for why this is happening is that the keepers of the tradition have faded from the community's consciousness. The knowledge and experience of Utah musicians, who have dedicated their lives to fulfilling their community's needs for dance, are rarely validated on the community level.

Dance historian Laraine Miner revives the old-time dance repertoire for monthly community dances in Salt Lake County. Photo by Craig R. Miller, 1999.

Oak City has an unbroken legacy of community dancing that dates back to the founding of the town. Afton Dutson (seated at her piano) says her great-grandfather played for some of the earliest dances. To this day, the popular Oak City Quadrille is traditionally called by a member of the Bryce Finlinson family. Community dances are held often and for almost any reason. Another Oak City dance tradition that has been handed down through the years requires any older unmarried brothers of a wedding couple to dance in a pig trough which is hauled inside during the wedding dance party! Photo by Craig R. Miller, 1998.

At the close of her 1983 thesis, Laraine Miner reports that her dance informants "were for the most part elderly people in a society that worships its youth and turns a deaf ear to the stories and rich heritage of its elderly population."[51] It is not therefore surprising that the old-time Utah dance and music repertoire has become a display of self-conscious nostalgia or been relegated to less publicly visible venues. In short, the repertoire no longer functions as a symbol of the region, the culture or the LDS religion.

But the very fact that the repertoire exists at all proves that it still fulfills a cultural need for Mormon people. In fact, the old-time repertoire continues to function on three important levels that include the community, the family and the individual. For some communities, old-time dance provides a link to history and heritage and functions to unite neighbors and strangers in a celebration of shared values. For families, the old-time repertoire can serve as a symbol of family identity that is perpetuated along with an instrument inherited from a beloved grandparent or a story of ancestors who settled the frontier. For individuals lucky enough to have experienced the golden years of social dance in the West, this living heritage of music and dance serves as a reminder of loved ones, past visions and days gone by.

The music and dance heritage of the Mormon West is not yet lost; it is just under-appreciated and neglected. The real purpose of this study is to identify this heritage, place it in its historical and contemporary context and provide the tools to encourage its perpetuation. Perhaps by discovering its historical importance to the region, those who still cherish these traditions will hold them even more dear and work even harder to pass them along to the next generation.

Through the Folk Arts Apprenticeship Program, Cory Webster learns the old-time repertoire from Pattie Richards, daughter of Uintah Basin musicians Leroy and Weltha Thacker. Photo by Annie Hatch, 1994.

Merle K. Shumway holds the 1988 Utah Governor's Folk Art Award which she received for keeping her family's heritage of music and dance alive in Provo, Utah County. Photo by Craig R. Miller, 1991.

There are many who know nothing of the role music and dance have played in firing the imaginations and sustaining the spirits of people across the generations. They will never understand this heritage by only reading about it. They need to learn the dances, hear the music and experience the atmosphere and feeling of community that is created through dance. Only then will they see the beauty and understand the value of perpetuating these old-time traditions. If rejuvenated, this is a heritage that can provide spiritual nourishment and enjoyment for today's generations and for generations yet to come.

Sources Cited

1. Laraine Miner, *Early Utah Dance* (M.A. thesis, California State University, Hayward, 1983), 18.

2. "Pioneer Recreation Centers," quoted in Kate B. Carter, ed. *Our Pioneer Heritage*, 20 vols. (Salt Lake City: International Society, Daughters of Utah Pioneers, 1958-1977), 8:427-28.

3. Jessee Belle Stirling Pack, Autobiography, in Carter, *Our Pioneer Heritage*, 6:32.

4. *Woman's Exponent* (August 15, 1878) 7:41. See also Edward W. Tullidge, *The Women of Mormondom* (New York: Tullidge & Crandall, 1877), 32.

5. Benjamin F. Johnson, *My Life's Review* (Independence, Missouri: Zion's Printing and Publishing Co., 1947), 30.

6. "To the Editor of *Times and Seasons*," *Times and Seasons* (March 1, 1844), 5:459.

7. Ibid., 460.

8. Helen Whitney, "Scenes and Incidents in Nauvoo," *Woman's Exponent* 11 (November 15, 1882), 90.

9. Elizabeth Haven Barlow, Autobiography, in Carter, *Our Pioneer Heritage*, 19:319.

10. "Early Bands and Leaders," in Carter, *Our Pioneer Heritage*, 20:71-72.

11. William Clayton, *Journal of William Clayton* (New York: Arno Press, 1973), 5-8.

12. Thomas Kane, quoted in B. H. Roberts, *Comprehensive History of the Church*, 6 vols., (Provo, Utah: Corporation of the President, The Church of Jesus Christ of Latter-day Saints, 1965), 3:84.

13. Joseph Hovey. *Autobiography*, typescript, BYU Special Collections, 43.

14. Amber Maria Hamson Doyle, "Portraits of Yesterday," in Carter, *Our Pioneer Heritage*, 17:163.

15. Mary Culmer Simmons, "The Year 1868," in Carter, *Our Pioneer Heritage*, 12:31-32.

16. "Social Activities of Early Cache Valley," in Carter, *Our Pioneer Heritage*, 8:546.

17. Aroet Hale, *Autobiography*, typescript, BYU Special Collections, 17.

18. Eliza R. Snow, quoted in "Utah Recreation Centers," in Carter, *Our Pioneer Heritage*, 8:433.

19. "Utah Recreation Centers," in Carter, *Our Pioneer Heritage*, 8:455.

20. Dean Chelsley Robinson, "Millard County," in Carter, *Our Pioneer Heritage*, 8:473.

21. Susa Young Gates, *The Life Story of Brigham Young* (New York: The Macmillan Company, 1930), 253.

22. Rachel Emma Woolley Simmons, "Journal of Rachel Woolley Simmons," in *Heart Throbs of the West*, comp. Kate B. Carter, 12 vols. (Salt Lake City: Daughters of the Utah Pioneers, 1939-51), 11:165.

23. "Social Hall," in Carter, *Our Pioneer Heritage*, 5:216.

24. Deseret News, "Returned Missionaries' Party in the Social Hall," quoted in Carter, *Our Pioneer Heritage*, 8:446.

25. Mena Hasler Sorenson, "Sanpete County," in Carter, *Our Pioneer Heritage*, 8:477.

26. Kenner C. Kartchner, *Frontier Fiddler*, ed. Larry V. Shumway (Tucson: University of Arizona Press, 1990), 37, 82, 166, and 186.

27. C. J. Arthur, "Iron County," in Carter, *Our Pioneer Heritage*, 20:12.

28. "Paragonah," in Carter, *Our Pioneer Heritage*, 20:12.

29. "Kane County," in Carter, *Our Pioneer Heritage*, 20:14.

30. "True to the Faith," in Carter, *Our Pioneer Heritage*, 15:195.

31. Gates, 266.

32. Mosiah Hancock. *Autobiography*, typescript, BYU Special Collections, 14.

33. Miner, 15.

34. "In the Chase Home," in Carter, *Our Pioneer Heritage*, 8:445.

35. Miner, 7-8.

36. Davis Bitton, "These Licentious Days: Dancing Among the Mormons," *Sunstone* 2, no. 1 (Spring, 1977): 17.

37. Bitton, 23.

38. Bitton, 25.

39. "Saltair Beach," in Carter, *Our Pioneer Heritage*, 2:152

40. Kenner C. Kartchner, *Frontier Fiddler*, ed. Larry V. Shumway (Tucson: University of Arizona Press, 1990).

41. Renee J. LaPerriere, *The Varsouvienne in the Southwestern United States* (M.A. thesis, Sam Houston State University, Huntsville, Texas, 1995), 11-12.

42. Robert Stevenson, *Music in Mexico: A Historical Survey* (Thomas Y. Crowell Company, Apollo edition, 1971), 206-7.

43. Lloyd Shaw, *The Round Dance Book* (Caldwell, Idaho: Caxton Printers, 1948), 117.

44. Shaw, 114.

45. Roger Lax & Frederick Smith, eds., *The Great Song Thesaurus* (New York: Oxford University Press, second edition, 1989), 301.

46. Lax & Smith, 368.

47. Lax & Smith, 331, 219.

48. Lax & Smith, 257.

49. Lax & Smith, 354.

50. Lax & Smith, 208.

51. Miner, 50.

Index of Individuals, Locations, and Dance Halls

References in photographs and captions are indicated by bold page numbers.

Aaron Nelson's String Group: **12**
Allred, Mabel: **40**
Altamont: **25**
Alton: 42, 46
American Fork: 21
Anderson, Reva: **44**
Antelope Island State Park: **4**

Barlow, Carole: **2, 2**
Beaver: 18
Big Apple Outdoor Dance Hall: **7**
Billy Van's Dance Hall: **34**
Bingham Canyon: 53
Bitton, Davis, 31
Black, Verna: 2, **2, 42**
Bluffdale: 2, 43, **29, 40**
Booth, Jim, 41
Brigham City Dance Hall: **29**
Brigham Young University (BYU): 2, 6, 8

Call, Bonnie: **4**
Camp, Carl: 19
Capitol Reef National Park: 43, **35**
Carling, Maryette: 2, **42**
Carter, Robert & Lyndia: 3
Cedar City: 3, 23, 50, **50**
Chamberlain, Mercy: 45, 46, **45, 47**
Chamberlain, Thomas: **46, 47**
Chase Home Museum of Utah Folk Arts: **28**
Chase, Isaac: 28
Chidester, Sam: 2, 3, 43, 49, **1, 35**
Christensen, Christian, Harold, Lew, Peter, Willam: **29**
Clark, J. Shirley: 37, **38**
Cobblecrest Outdoor Dance Hall: 2, **2**
Colonia Dublan, Mexico: 37
Colorado City, Arizona: 2, 43, **42**
Cosy Corner Outdoor Dance Hall: **35**
Cox, Allan and Twila: **44**
Cox, Myrna: **44**
Crawford, Dan and Louis: **15**
Culmer, Mary: 17

Dance Hall Rock: 51, **51, 52**
David Smith Orchestra: 33
Dutson, Afton: **54**

Edison, Carol: 3
Enoch Orchestra: 49
Enterprise: **16, 26**
Enterprise Orchestra: **16, 26**
Escalante: 51
Esplin, Ruby: **44**

Fairview: 20
Fillmore: 19
Flanigan, Ellsworth (Sagebrush): 3, 50
Fiddlers Green Dance Hall: 20
Finlinson, Bryce: **54**
First Family Orchestra, Gladys, Lester, Vernon, Wallace: **Cover, 30**
Flake, Charlie and James: 20
Flake Brothers' Hall: 20

Garfield Beach: 23
Garner, Catherine: **1, 4**
Gates, Susa Young: 23
Grant, Jedediah M.: 20
Geneva: 21
Gifford Family: **36, 36, 42**
Greaves, Afton: 53
Grouse Creek: 42
Gunlock: **30**

Hale, Aroet: 17
Hancock, Mosiah and Levi: 24
Harrison, Heber and Ellen: **21**
Hastings, Pete: **36**
Heaps, Lell: 3, **1, 35**
Hepworth, Charles: **47**
Hermitage, Ogden Canyon: **31**
Hidden Lake Outdoor Dance Hall: 45
Hooper: 2, 43, **1, 4**
Hooper Hometown Players: **1**
Humphries, Ammron: **47**
Hurricane: **40**

Jessop, Joseph Lymon: **27**
Jessop, Rosy and Ellen: 2, **27, 29**
John Perry Orchestra: 3, 50
Johnson, Benjamin E.: 12
Johnston, Genevieve: **1, 4**
Jones, Keith: 3
Jukebox Cave: 53

Kanab: 50
Kanarraville: **2**
Kane, Col. Thomas: 16
Kanosh: **9**
Kartchner, Kenner C.: 2, 36, 49, **10, 20, 22**
Keith Jones: 3
Kimball, Heber C.: 17, 20, 28
Kimberly Dance Hall: **18**
Kingston: **51**
Kirtland, Ohio: 12
Kite, Margie: **4**

Lagoon Dancing Pavilion: **39**
Layton: **38**
Lazy Bar Ranch: **48**
Leigh, Beth: 50
Lincoln Beach: 21
Logan: **38**
Long Valley: 42, 45
Lyman, Amasa: 20
Lynne Clark Photographic Studios: 3

Mace, Hiram: 19
Matthews, John: 18
Midvale: 53
Miner, Laraine: 3, 8, 28, 54, **2, 54**
Mormon Battalion: 16
Moroni: 20
Mt. Carmel: 23
Mt. Pleasant: 20
Mt. Timpanogos: **Table of Contents page**

Nauvoo: 14, 15, 24
Nielsen, Niels Peter: 20
Nisson, Quentin: 41, **42, 43**

Oak City: **54**
Orderville: 42, 45, 46, 49, **10, 26, 44, 45, 46, 47**
Orderville Orchestra: 42, 45, 46, **44, 45**

Pack, Jesse Belle Stirling: 11
Palisade Outdoor Dance Hall: 53, **53**
Paragonah: 23
Parker, Ralph (Tex): **48, 49**
Parker Sisters: 2
Penny, Norma: **44**
Peterson, Clinton: **35**
Pine Valley: 14
Pinto: 21
Pitchfork Band: **36**

Pitt, William: 16
Pleasant Grove: 21
Poverty Bench Boys Band: **35**
Provo: **25**
Pulsipher, Harriett: 17
Purple Haze Outdoor Dance Hall: 53, **51**

Reber, Desie: **36**
Rendezvous Outdoor Dance Hall: 53
Richards, Pattie: **Cover, 8, 55**
Rooftop Gardens: 53
Rouche, Vida Adams: **38**
Rulon C. Allred Building: 27
Russell Brothers Band: **17**

St. George: 4, 6, **12, 17, 18**
St. George–Pine Valley Orchestra: **18**
St. Johns, Arizona: **10**
Saltair: 21, 33, **32, 33, Back Cover**
Salt Lake Bowery: 21
Salt Lake City: 19, 20, 28, 31, **13, 21, 26**
Salt Lake Theater: 20, 27
Salt Palace: 26
Seegmiller, Lulabelle: **36**
Shady Dell Outdoor Dance Hall: **3**
Shaw, Lloyd: 39
Shumway, Kirsten: 25
Shumway, Larry: 2, 36, **3, 25**
Shumway, Merle: 35, 36, 43, 49, **3, 10, 20, 25, 55**
Shumway, Nathan: **25**
Simmons, Rachel: 19
Smith, Joseph: 15
Snow, Eliza R.: 18
Snowflake, Arizona: 20, 35, 36, 42, 43
Social Hall: 19, 20, 27, **20**
Sorensen, Binnie: **47**
Spencer, Howard: 45, **45**
Spring City: 20
Springdale: 15
S. S. Showboat: 53
Starlight Outdoor Dance Hall: 53, **41**

Tait, Bernard: **44**
Tait, Berneta: **47**
Tait Family Band: 49
Tait, Lyn: **47**
Tait, Rena: 46, 49, **44, 46**
Tait, Val: **44**
Taylor, John: 14
Teasdale Cultural Hall: **34**
Tex Parker and His Wasatch Buckaroos: **48, 49**
Thacker Family, LeRoy and Weltha: 2, 41, 49, **24, 25, 55**
Toquerville: **41**
Torrey: **7**

Uintah Basin: 2, 41, 43, 49, **24, 25, 55**

Warm Springs Resort: 19, **19**
Wasatch Mountain Club: **Cover, 31**
Washington City: 49, 43
Washington Orchestra: 49
Webster, Cory: **8, 55**
Wendover: 53
Whitney, Elizabeth: 12
Winter Quarters: 11, 16
Wood, Iva Williams: 2

Young, Brigham: 11, 15, 16, 17, 23, 27, 28, 33
Youngbood, Claude: **10**

Zion National Park: 42, **Cover**